Fifty Years Together

Riding the promises of Vatican II through five decades
of what felt like coincidences in our favor.

In every life there are chance events that make all the difference;
that sponsor directions not foreseen—coincidences in our favor.
Another name for this is grace.

Fifty Years Together

Eros with Wrinkles

In memory of Evelyn Eaton Whitehead

JAMES WHITEHEAD

For Keith & Connie

Good Memories —

Jim Whitehead

© 2022 by James Whitehead

Book design by the HK Scriptorium

Cover art by Jane Pitz. The Chinese character (*ren*), literally two persons together, means benevolence or the virtue of humanity. It is embossed on our wedding rings.

ISBN 9798844061042

For

Evelyn Eaton Whitehead

August 22, 1938 — November 16, 2020

Companion for Fifty Years

Loving God
You have shared with us
her life.
Before she was ours,
she was yours.
For all that she has given us
to make us who we are,
for that of her
which lives and
grows in each of us,
and for her life
that in your love
will never end,
we give you thanks.
—Jane Pitz

Contents

The Palmer House Chicago

That love between man and woman which is neither planned nor willed, but somehow imposes itself upon human beings. (Encyclical of Pope Benedict XVI, *God Is Love*, § 3)

Easter Sunday, 1968

Traveling from Minneapolis to St. Louis, where I was finishing an MA in theology, I decided to stop in Chicago to visit a classmate from years past. Taking the airport bus into the city and the Palmer House Hotel I was not sure I would even recognize Evelyn Eaton after four years apart.

We had only meant to get caught up on each other's lives. No hint of romance or other expectations for two persons fully engaged in their separate lives. Certainly no intent of falling in love, but fall we did. Sitting in the lobby of the hotel, we talked and then talked some more. We could not finish the conversation. I decided to delay my return to St. Louis until the next day and called a fellow Jesuit to let me stay at his house overnight. The next day Evelyn and I talked some more before I returned to O'Hare.

We were smitten. Thirty-two years later Pope Benedict XVI got it about right when he described "that love between man and woman which is neither planned nor willed, but somehow imposes itself upon human beings."

Lost in Thought

Seven years earlier our paths had first crossed at St. Louis University, where we arrived to pursue an MA in philosophy. For the next three years we took many of the same courses, used the same library, crossed the same campus, with little interaction. We were both in our early twenties and intent on our own careers, scholars in the making. Lost in thought.

In 1964, after finishing our studies we went our separate ways: Evelyn to Appalachia to continue working as a Glenmary Sister with the people there, myself to South Korea to teach in a small seminary college staffed by American Jesuits. The Glenmary Sisters were a new group of Sisters who called themselves "home missioners" committed to serving the people in Appalachia, known as "no priest land USA." When Evelyn joined this group in 1956 as an eighteen-year-old she was one year older than the congregation itself. Through the mid-1960s Evelyn moved back and forth between Big Stone Gap, Virginia, and Chicago, where Appalachians were migrating as the coal industry began to contract. In Chicago Evelyn helped establish the Appalachian Study Center, which welcomed those who wanted to learn more about this disadvantaged group.

This was the era when Catholic Sisters were shifting from their traditional role staffing parish schools to engaging in questions of social advocacy and social justice. Instead of living in large convents, they often found housing in apartments in troubled neighborhoods. *The Saturday Evening Post*, in the summer of 1966, published a photo essay entitled "The New Nuns," which featured the Glenmary Sisters, with Evelyn's photo on p. 27. The next year Studs Terkel published *Division Street America*, which included essays on various citizens of Chicago who were engaged in the turmoil and creativity of those days. Chapter 7 was titled "Sister Evelyn, Age 26."

For myself, South Korea was an exciting change from years of study. American Jesuits had been asked to staff a seminary in this country, which was still struggling to recover from the war that only a decade earlier had torn the nation apart. As we instructed these young Koreans in philosophy and theology—Western ideas, all—we began to question our role in the heart of Asia. What were we Americans attempting to accomplish? These were the questions that were just being surfaced at the Second Vatican Council taking place during these same years and led me a decade later to begin my study of Asian religions.

Unable to answer these questions, we did rejoice in some very practical liturgical changes that transpired during my final year in Korea. In the summer of 1966, these changes came to Kwangju. One Sunday that summer, the liturgy was suddenly recited in the Korean language instead of in Latin. For the first time parishioners could understand the prayers of the Eucharist. As they entered the chapel they were encouraged to abandon the genuflection that had felt so alien to them and instead offer a deep bow—a gesture of devotion that had been in their bones for centuries. The Eucharist in the vernacular with a deep bow replacing an awkward genuflection: Vatican II had come to Kwangju.

Evelyn and I lived our twenties during the creative turmoil of the 1960s, but we were children of the 1950s with its solid if insular faith. Marrying in 1970 we rode the promises of Vatican II through five decades of what felt like coincidences in our favor.

Catholics in the 1950s

As the 1950s began, American Catholics stood on the cusp of a new era. Returning soldiers—offspring of Italian, Irish, and Polish immigrants—were entering college in large numbers, the first of their families to seek higher education. The next generation would continue this upward social mobility as Catholics replaced their outsider status for that of engaged citizens.

The 1950s represented the final decade in which American Catholics would abide in a sheltered existence, at arm's length from the culture and the world. Flannery O'Connor judged that "the Catholic in this country suffers from a parochial aesthetic and a cultural insularity." During this decade many American Catholics continued to live contentedly in their own insular neighborhoods. They often preferred to remain in areas with their own church, school, and hospital. Mary Gordon, in her novel *Final Payments,* has Isabel describe her own father's contentment. "It was natural for him not to want to leave the neighborhood where the church was so predominant it did not need to be upheld."

Catholics at mid-century were formed in a faith defined by the questions and answers in the *Baltimore Catechism.* The Legion of Decency made clear which films were acceptable, which condemned. Many families, including ours, posted this list on the refrigerator as a reminder. For those with more scholarly interests, the Index of Forbidden Books still prevailed. Catholic rhetoric was harsh in its warning about the perils of association with non-Catholics. Flannery O'Connor defended her use of misfits and freaks in her short stories: writers "must often tell 'perverse' stories to 'shock' a morally blind world." Evelyn Waugh had described his intent in writing *Brideshead Revisited*: "to trace the divine purpose in a pagan world."

Catholic identity was clear and exclusive: clear in doctrine and devotion; exclusive as Catholics separated themselves from the surrounding environment of "non-Catholics." Graham Greene had described "the hard edges of Catholicism" that gave a satisfying clarity and confidence in the midst of the upheavals and turmoil in the world. Gordon's *Final Payments*: "Protestants, it said, thought about moral issues, drank water and ate crackers, took care to exercise and had a notion that charity was synonymous with good works. Catholics, on the other hand, thought about eternity, drank wine and smoked cigars, were sometimes extravagant, but knew that charity was a fire in the heart of God and never confused it with the Protestant invention, philanthropy."

In 1951 the Catholic presence in American culture had suddenly turned up the volume. Bishop Fulton J. Sheen, resplendent in his red episcopal robes, cast his telegenic figure into the homes of millions of Catholics in his new TV show. This was something to be proud of. That same year a brash twenty-six-year-old Catholic published the book *God, Man and Yale*. In it William Buckley proclaimed his arrival on the cultural scene with his "I am Catholic; hear me roar."

The following year was a bonanza for Catholic publishing. The French Catholic novelist Francois Mauriac was awarded the Nobel Prize for Literature. Dorothy Day published her memoir, *The Long Loneliness,* and Flannery O'Connor saw her first novel, *Wise Blood,* into print. Meanwhile Thomas Merton's *The Seven Storey Mountain* continued to be a literary best-seller. The book in its first year (1948–1949) had sold 600,000 copies, but *The New York Times* initially chose not to include it in its best-seller list, deeming it "a religious book."

Thomas Merton and Dorothy Day stand as pivotal authors in the shift in the Catholic imagination that was emerging at mid-century. When Merton turned his attention to social structures after a decade in the Trappist monastery, Dorothy Day had already been spending herself in challenging these structures for a quarter century. In the course of the 1950s and 1960s they would together foster a new direction for Catholic faith: a more socially engaged and optimistic persuasion.

Dueling Soundtracks for the 1960s

The decade had begun all charm. On the morning of November 9, 1960, Catholics awoke to the news that one of theirs had been elected president of the United States. John F. Kennedy quickly set about spinning a web of enchantment (code name: Camelot) from his inaugural speech—"Ask not what the country can do for you, but what you can do for your country"—to the creation of the Peace Corps (1961), to the challenge to put a person on the moon during the decade. Three years after his election Kennedy was assassinated in Dallas, and Camelot ended in disenchantment.

Eugene McCarraher ("Speaking Love to Power," *Commenweal* [February 2020] pp. 22-23) sums up the cultural tension of this decade: "the countercultural revolution in manners and morals cleared space for feminism, ecological sensitivity, and sexual liberation. Of course the custodians of traditional mores take the opposite line: the counterculture was a sexual and hallucinogenic pandemonium that prefigured our decadence."

The 1960s was a decade that was read in contradictory ways. A time of disenchantment—the multiple assassinations, the escalating war in Vietnam—that many experienced during these tumultuous years. But for many this decade of enchantment—the excitement of the Second Vatican Council, the civil rights legislation, the onset of environmental concerns—rendered the decade an extraordinary time.

One of the dueling soundtracks for the decade was Don McLean's cryptic ballad "American Pie" (1971). Associated with the death of Buddy Holly in 1959, the song tried to name a larger loss. *"The three men I admire the most, the father, son and holy ghost, they took the last train to the coast, the day the music died."* Poet Adrienne Rich in 1969 offered her feminist assessment of the previous decade: "The old masters, the old sources, haven't a clue what we're about, shivering here in the half-dark 'sixties.'"

For some Catholics of a certain age the 1960s seemed like a time when a more innocent era was giving way to a period of moral collapse and the debut of the culture wars still being waged today. They can trace a through-line from the government's approval of the birth control pill in 1960 to the moral excesses of Woodstock in the summer of 1969 to Roe v. Wade in 1973. In April 2019 the ninety-two-year-old "retired" pope, Benedict XVI, penned a six-thousand-word letter, lamenting the changes in society and inside the church beginning in the 1960s that led to what he called an "all-out sexual freedom."

Conservative writer Joseph Bottum explains the disenchantment of many Catholics that arose in that period. "One understanding of the sexual revolution—the best I think—is an enormous turn against the meaningfulness of sex." For Bottum and others, "the actual effect was to disconnect sex from what previous eras had thought the deep stuff of life: God, birth, death, heaven, hell, the moral structures of the universe, and all the rest." In his judgment, "the sexual revolution led to a disenchanting [of] the Western understanding of sexual intercourse."

A traditional enchantment of sexuality had meant respecting the sacredness of sexual sharing; shame was the guardian virtue meant to kept sex in the bedroom of the married. A new sense of freedom and even promiscuity threatened this understanding. David Brooks comments: "One of the principal outcomes of the sexual revolution was to establish that sex is just like any other social interaction—nothing taboo or sacred about it."

Abuses certainly abounded in this decade as a younger generation moved away from an inherited caution about sexuality; pornography and promiscuity flourished. But for many Catholics the decade of the 1960s was a period of exciting and positive change.

The second song was Simon and Garfunkel's "Bridge over Troubled Waters." Published in 1970, their song saw things otherwise. *"When darkness comes and pain is all around I will lay me down like a bridge over troubled waters."* The dirge of "American Pie" gave way to the Beatles' "Hey Jude" (*"take a sad song and make it better,"* 1968) that shifted the culture's music toward enchantment. Still the widespread disenchantment loosed in the decade continued to contest with cultural events of a more encouraging cast.

Before the decade began a young African-American man had fled to France to escape the racism in his own country. As James Baldwin tells it in the documentary "I Am Not Your Negro," he could find solace in Paris but could not speak Black truth to White power from such a remove. Returning to America, he wrote *Notes on a Native Son* (1955); then in 1963, *The Fire Next Time*. On August 28 of that year, Martin Luther King delivered his most famous speech, "I Have a Dream," at the March on Washington, galvanizing millions to a deeper appreciation of racism in American life. Baldwin's words, King's dream, and Muhammed Ali's actions—renaming himself and rejecting the military draft—became an early iteration of Black Lives Matter.

That same year, a marine biologist by the name of Rachel Carson published *Silent Spring*, which laid out the destructive force of pesticides like DDT that remain in the soil and water with long-lasting toxic effects. ("Silent Spring" refers to a spring when these pesticides have finally silenced the songbirds.) Carson's blend of scientific analysis and poetic prose roused Americans for the first time to an awareness that nature is not an inanimate reservoir to be endlessly exploited but a living organism to which humans also belong. In an earlier book, *The Edge of the Sea*, Carson mused on that meeting of ocean and land—"that enchanted place on the threshold of the sea." Carson's work initiated the environmental movement.

The following year, Betty Friedan's *The Feminine Mystique* stirred many women to "the problem that had no name"—women's dissatisfaction with the cultural constraints that kept them homebound, awaiting the return of the bread-winning husband while denied other engagements in the world. Her outrage took up where Simone de Beauvoir's *The Second Sex* (1949) had left off, which had taken up where the suffrage movement earlier in the century had left off. Sexuality was a special issue of this new age of feminism, with women desiring more control over their own bodies. Today's #MeToo Movement belongs to this tradition. All these movements made, for many Americans, an enchanting era.

"Children of God"—All Grown up

"Children of God" is an enchanting image: the comfort of being cared for and protected by God as loving parent. Yet when this metaphor is placed within a hierarchical church structure Catholics may be encouraged to see themselves as life-long children subjected to the direction of their "fathers"—the parental clergy.

The bishops at the Second Vatican Council (1962–1965) signaled a sea change in their vision of lay Christians when they began the important document on the church (*Lumen Gentium*, Light of the World) not with a discussion of the hierarchy of bishops and priests but with reflections on the church as "the people of God." This ancient term—"people," *laos* in the Greek of the New Testament (from which we derive "laity")—was meant to remind lay Catholics of their importance in the life and ministry of the church.

The bishops were encouraging lay Catholics to turn away from traditional and passive self-understandings (as the cynic suggests, "to pray, pay, and obey"). The key to a more adult sense of self was a respect for one's conscience. At the beginning of the 1960s conscience most often meant the willingness to obey, to follow the instructions of clerical leaders called "fathers." By the end of the decade, conscience had come to mean the developed capacity to discern. This entailed the discovery of one's own gifts and vocation and the courage to follow this inner guidance. This meant not only developing one's conscience, but the courage to follow it.

The church's sudden investment in lay Catholics as spiritual adults seemed abrupt to many. Only in retrospect can we see how this development had been quietly evolving for decades. A first step had been a book on Catholic marriage by a married Catholic in Germany. Church teaching on marriage had until then always been promoted by unmarried clergy. Dietrich von Hildebrand in his book had shifted the focus of matrimony from procreation to the mutuality and intimacy of the couple itself.

In the decades before the 1960s two spiritual movements in the church encouraged lay Catholics to take a more emotional engagement in their faith. The *Cursillo,* a spiritual retreat that had begun in Spain, presented a format for lay Catholics to experience, often for the first time, a style of prayer and discussion that emphasized faith as more than an intellectual assent to doctrines. Many lay Catholic men have testified that the experience of a *Cursillo* had given them for the first time a genuine adult engagement in their faith.

During the 1940s and 1950s, married Catholics began to gather in groups as part of the *Christian Family Movement* (CFM), with the goal of rendering their faith more alive within their own families. In the early 1960s, the *Marriage Encounter* movement offered weekend retreats for married couples with the focus being the couple's own intimacy. These gatherings were led by a married couple plus a chaplain priest—the first time that lay Catholics were seen as capable of religious leadership.

All these movements, developing over several decades, prepared lay Catholics to more fully appreciate what adult faith, both in the parish and in their own marriages, should look like. A decade before the Council a new Catholic magazine, *Jubilee*, printed its first edition. Its founders were two lay Catholics who had been friends of Thomas Merton in their college years. Their goal for the journal as to "bridge the gap between religion and culture by bringing into view a new world in which it is the privilege of the Christian to cooperate with God in restoring all things in Christ."

As we sat in the lobby of the Palmer House in Chicago on Easter Sunday, the turmoil of that fateful year—1968—had begun. Martin Luther King had just been assassinated. Bobby Kennedy's death was only a few months away. In July the Vatican would publish a document—*Humanae Vitae*—that forbade Catholics from using any kind of artificial birth control. At year's end the monk and popular writer Thomas Merton was in Bangkok for a conference on world religions when his life was cut short at age fifty-four. The end of something or the beginning?

It would take us most of 1969 to finally find our way together. On a very cold January day in 1970 we married in Bond Chapel at the University of Chicago. So we began.

Jim and Evelyn in 2003; photo by Rita Koehler (copyright)

Part One

"Behold, I am making something new"
(Isaiah 43:19)

CHAPTER ONE

Dancing in the Streets— The 1970s

There were rousing liturgies with dancers in the aisles, their bodies praising the Lord. Participants were vigorously re-examining their vocations, ministries, lifestyles. People were falling in and out of love. Eros was in the air.

Four months into our marriage I began teaching my first course at the Institute for Pastoral Studies at Loyola University, Chicago. The course was contracted as a one-off experiment but stretched into a career of forty-five years for Evelyn and myself. The theme of the course was a theology of hope. Indeed.

That first course had ninety participants, nearly all priests and nuns, with only two lay persons in the group. Over the next two decades that ratio would dramatically change as laity came to dominate the program. My lecturing was still in the old style of the professor talking at great length with a question or two at the end. That too would change as the Institute reimagined its adventure not as a gathering of passive "students" but of adult participants.

In the summer of 1970 each of us was in the midst of a major pivot. Evelyn was finishing her studies in Human Development at the University of Chicago and looking for a focus for her dissertation. I had just completed an MA in theology and was pivoting from my twelve years as a Jesuit to a life where a living wage suddenly became a lively issue.

When the course ended we left Chicago and headed for Big Stone Gap, Virginia, the heart of Appalachia, where Evelyn would explore topics for her research. In mid-August we drove on to Harvard and our housing at the Center for the Study of World Religions. For the next three years, except for our summers in Chicago, we lived in a cocoon of scholarship, far from the practical concerns of church life. This would give us the space to find the "together" in our new life.

A Holding Environment

Each summer we would return to Loyola University in Chicago to continue teaching in the Institute for Pastoral Studies. The Institute had begun the summer of 1964 as the Vatican Council was nearing its close. Over the next several years, scholars from Europe who were versed in the liturgical changes sponsored by the Council arrived in Chicago to educate Americans in these profound changes.

For six weeks each summer through the 1970s three hundred Catholics came together in exciting, challenging explorations of the meaning of vocation, friendship and intimacy, and community. Discussions would often continue through lunch and dinner, which were taken together at the University dining hall.

In a lecture that marked a half century of the Institute's life, I tried to capture the energy and creativity of those early days: "Each summer 300 people gathered at Lake Shore campus, in a vital community: living, eating, celebrating liturgy in the same place for six weeks. Participants were overwhelmingly vowed religious and clergy. For nearly all of us this was a new way of experiencing Christian community."

It was a time of intense personal renewal. On a more personal note, this is where Evelyn and I found our shared vocation. In those first years we taught separate courses, Evelyn, developmental psychology, and myself, Christian spirituality. Quickly we came to realize that we were born to teach together and to do it here. This is close to the best grace we have ever received. From those days forward this has been our spiritual home; when we travel it is to here we return.

The legacy of those first years was the Institute as a holding environment where adults come to discern the shifting shape of their vocation and ministry. British psychologist D. W. Winnicott had coined the term "holding environment" to describe a context where a parent—an authority figure—steps away from the immediate presence with her child, allowing space for the child to play in a more independent-like setting. Not being told what to do or what to think, the child indulges in a new sense of freedom and attentiveness. She dares to think thoughts she hadn't dared before. It was this freedom of "the children of God" that permeated the Institute during the 1970s, allowing participants to concentrate and play in new and creative ways.

During these same years the faculty were crafting the

distinctive style of adult education that is second nature now: a shift from lectures of experts to an arena of shared ideas and contested visions. Not a theology department but a community of pastoral reflection and discernment. This may be IPS's most enduring legacy: a learning community where adults develop skills of discernment, grow their vocations, where "young people see visions and old people dream dreams"(Acts 2:17).

Sojourn at Harvard

What were we doing at Harvard? It seems like a long way from the holding environment of Loyola. The explanation lay in my three years in South Korea (1964–1967) where I had come into a world far beyond the comfortable Western Catholicism I had been born into. It would have been easy—too easy—to continue my study of theology and complete a PhD in this Western discipline. Beyond our world of Catholic thought, which some days could seem quite parochial, was another world; what was the Spirit of God about there?

While Evelyn was writing her dissertation on Catholics' acceptance of the new directions of Vatican II, I turned to the study of the religions of China. (I had been told that before continuing my study of Korea I should give some attention to its neighbor China. Alas, "some attention" turned out to be an unending adventure.)

My goal was not to become an expert either on the Korean culture or the Chinese language (thirty years old being a bit late for such folly) but to rub up against these worlds until they began to influence my own thinking. This might be the Korean emotion of *han*—an angry resentment inherited from centuries of abuse by their neighbors—or the Chinese concept of *qi* as vital energy that circulates through the world, animating and healing whatever it touches.

Besides the study of the Chinese language and history I dove into the history of Daoism in a course taught by an eccentric Chinese scholar by the name of Achilles Fong. There we dallied with the ancient Daoist Zhuangzi, who had asked, "What is the use of the useless?" referring to trees so gnarled that no carpenter thought of using them for building and the crippled person unfit for recruitment as cannon fodder). The brilliant sinologist Benjamin Schwarz took us through the intellectual history of China from Confucius in 500 BCE to Wang Yangming, a contemporary of Luther, Ignatius Loyola, and Theresa of Avila in the 1500s.

But my main instructor who became the director of my dissertation was a Japanese professor, a Buddhist by the name of Masatoshi Nagatomi. When I chose the dissertation topic of a Buddhist story of a lay person who instead of following the traditional path to wisdom in a monastic vocation chose a married life immersed in everyday life, Nagatomi gently pointed out the similarity of my own journey from Jesuit scholar to married layman.

The doctoral program I was in was made to order for Jesuits or former Jesuits like myself who had already studied philosophy and theology and also spent three years in a foreign country. Six of us—three Jesuits who had taught in places like Pakistan and three former Jesuits who had taught in Korea and Japan—all of us a decade older than most of the other doctoral students, met regularly with Professor Nagatomi. On occasion he would remark on the similar style of study and writing by "you Jesuits." Each time I would correct him, reminding him that three of us were no longer in the Jesuit Order. And he would simply smile, a knowing Buddhist smile.

By the time I finished my PhD we were teaching at the University of Notre Dame, and I was invited to teach some courses on Buddhism. I chose not to take this path, sensing that I had accomplished what I had needed to do. With this grounding far afield from the Catholic tradition I turned back to pastoral theology, which was my true calling. As it had been with Korea years before, it seemed to me at the time that my affair with China was ending. Again, I was wrong.

During our years of teaching at Loyola participants from Korea and China kept arriving to take our courses and, to our great surprise, translate many of our books into their own languages. In 1994 we gave some lectures in Hong Kong that led to a short trip into the mainland. Soon we were teaching every fall semester at Fudan University in Shanghai. Over the next decade we published several textbooks on the comparative sociology of religion, leading us deeper into the ways of the Spirit in Asia.

The Focus of the 1970s: How to Adult?

The reforms of Vatican II had shuffled expectations about adult Christian maturing. "Vocation" had once been limited to lives of vowed religious and priesthood. Lay persons did not, strictly speaking, have vocations; apostolates perhaps, but not vocations. Now Catholics could picture their own vocations beginning in Baptism. We are all called; we are all gifted for service to others. Now Erik Erikson's question of identity—who am I?—could be reframed as a challenge of a vocation—what is God calling me to?

This raised another challenge to the Christian idea of vocation: are we called only once and for a lifetime? Or is God's call given us again and again? As we mature we become more able to hear invitations from God we had not noticed in our youth. It seems that God calls us repeatedly in a continuing conversation. A vocation is God revealing us to ourselves gradually; this could take a lifetime. But God revealing us to ourselves can be unsettling; it may bring us into a crisis.

If vocation now included new possibilities, so was Erik Erikson's question of intimacy: with whom shall I join my life? The answer might be religious life or marriage. Many participants had seemed to have settled questions of intimacy by joining themselves to a vocation that included celibacy. Now at Loyola they were making new friends and discussing over lunch questions that had been passed over in previous years.

In retrospect we realized the theme of intimacy was the single most important thread running through all our writing and lecturing. In the 1970s participants were hungry to sort out the promise of Vatican II. The arena of these conversations was protected space; only these six weeks. In the 1980s questions of intimacy were raised again, now in courses on sexuality.

Previously many participants had been counseled to keep things superficial, to avoid "particular friendships." Now they were keenly aware that this is the only kind of genuine friendship there is. Now there was a growing consensus about links between vocation and intimacy. Was celibacy the one fitting style of intimacy among ministers? Erikson had also emphasized the balance of intimacy and solitude—comfort with being alone. Participants were asked to assess this balance in their own lives.

Discussions returned to the eternal tension between our longing to be close to others and the jeopardy involved in such proximity. Will we be overwhelmed? Taken advantage of? Did we have enough confidence in own identity to risk an opinion, stick out your neck, expose your fragile self?

We invited participants to reflect on intimacy as "a web." Did this image evoke feelings of support? Or feelings of entrapment? Often women and men differed in their sense of comfort with this image. Erikson: "Intimacy gives the strength to sustain relationships, to outlast the ambiguities that cloud our attempts to be with others."

THE UNFOLDING CHALLENGES OF ADULT LIFE IN THE PSYCHOLOGY OF ERIK ERIKSON

IDENTITY—VOCATION

"Who am I ... called to become?"

Developed through our late teens and early twenties

Growing comfort with who I am; decisions about vocation

[CRISIS: threat and opportunity; can I risk my identity in relationships?]

INTIMACY

"Whom shall I be with?"; questions of belonging

Frequently settle in marriage or religious life. Friendship

[CRISIS: can I risk well-established bonds in changing a career, in new dreams?]

GENERATIVITY

> The impulse to care for others;
> Often expressed in having children, raising a family
> Also a movement of interiority: time to question where
>   I am
> [CRISIS: a challenge to move into leadership; try out new
>   dreams]

INTEGRITY

> Has my life made sense? Been worth the effort?
> Saying "yes" to my life as I have lived it.
> Embracing a good-enough self ...

Erikson's third challenge of adult maturing—generativity—named the desire to be creative, procreative. How am I called to care for the next generation—beginning a family or becoming a teacher or some other choice? For Erikson, this invitation drew us outward in care but also inward in a reflective mood he called "interiority." In our forties, after twenty years in a career, it may be time to re-examine the direction of my life. Slowing down, looking back over previous years I am aware that I have "more yesterdays than tomorrows." How shall I spend the years still given me? If I am to change directions for my life now is time to do it.

Erikson's genius lay in recognizing that each challenge is likely to come under threat before we can enter the next stage of maturing. A decision about vocation may elicit a crisis around intimacy. Or falling in love might scramble my firmly developed sense of vocation. What am I to do?

Crisis as Opportunity

The very term "crisis" evokes feelings of threat, but Erikson wrote of crises as those periods when a question— Who am I? Who will I be with? What kind of work should I do?—comes to urgent focus. One's stable sense of identity or purpose is suddenly destabilized. Erikson writes of "crucial periods of increased vulnerability and heightened potential"—a time not only of threat but of opportunity: we have the chance to re-examine and perhaps change a relationship or even a career.

Erikson's detailed definition is worth revisiting. "I shall present human growth from the point of view of the conflicts, inner and outer, which the vital personality weathers, re-emerging from each crisis with an increased sense of inner unity, with the increase of good judgment, and an increase in the capacity to 'do well' according to his own standards and to the standards of those who are significant to him" (*Identity, Youth, and Crisis*, 91).

"The strength of any one stage is tested by the necessity to transcend it in such a way that the individual can take chances in the next stage with what is most vulnerably precious in the previous one" (*Identity: Youth, and Crisis*, 74).

Evelyn sensed that this psychological orientation was a match for the instincts of Vatican II: *aggiornamento* (updating) meant change. Vocations mature, intimacy deepens, our sense of care becomes more nuanced. For some participants at Loyola, the program triggered a crisis: questions of identity, intimacy, and generative care arose in unsettling ways.

Crisis: Jacob Alone in the Dark, without a Clue

And Jacob was left alone. And someone wrestled with him until the breaking of the day. When the assailant saw that he did not prevail against Jacob he touched the hollow of his thigh and Jacob's thigh was put out of joint as he wrestled with him.

Then he said, "Let me go for the day is breaking." But Jacob said, "I will not let you go unless you bless me." And he said to him, "What is your name?" and he said, "Jacob." Then he said, "Your name shall no more be Jacob but Israel for you have struggled with God and with humans and have prevailed."

Then Jacob said, "Tell me your name," but the assailant responded, "Why do you keep asking about my name." And there he blessed him. So Jacob called the name of the place Peniel, for I have seen God face to face and yet my life is preserved.

The sun rose upon him as he passed Penuel, limping because of his thigh. Therefore to this day the Israelites do not eat the sinew of the hip which is upon the hollow of the thigh, because he touched the hollow of Jacob's thigh on the sinew of the hip. (Genesis 32:24-32)

Jacob is alone and in the dark. He is attacked by some shadowy figure that he will learn, with the light of dawn, is no ordinary wrestler but his own God. But this is a God who would struggle with us, is likely to wound us, perhaps even leaving us limping for a lifetime. A God unlike the figure in our catechism books.

Jacob struggles with God and prevails, but now carrying

a wound and a new name. After a night of struggle it dawns on Jacob who this combatant is. From this struggle Jacob comes into a new relationship with God, marked by a new identity and a new limp.

As we told this story again and again many individuals recognized such struggles in their life of faith and how a painful embrace led them to a new intimacy with a God with whom they have struggled.

A Zeitgeist in the Late 1970s

Looking back to the late 1970s we see a *Zeitgeist*—in Vatican-II language, a sign of the times—concerning the dynamics of adult change. This interest was first announced in William Bouwsma's "Christian Adulthood" essay in the *Daedalus Journal* (1976). His essay was followed the next year by Gail Sheehy's very popular *Patterns: Predictable Crises of Adult Life*. The two books that most engaged us were those of George Vaillant's *Adaptation to Life* (1977) and Daniel Levinson's *The Seasons of a Man's Life* (1978).

Vaillant was tracking a longitudinal study of Harvard undergraduates (The Grant Study) as these students matured from their twenties through the decades of their adult lives. This allowed Vaillant to chart different paths and pathologies of adult life. One example of the insight that Vaillant's study produced concerned the capacity to play as an adult resource.

> *It is hard to separate the capacity to trust from the capacity to play, for play is dangerous until we can trust both ourselves and our opponents to harness rage. In play we must trust enough and love enough to risk los-*

*ing without despair, to bear winning without guilt, and
to laugh at error without mockery. (Adaptation to Life,
77, 309)*

The psychological capacity to play, long outlasting
childhood, reinforces the strength that the Bible celebrates.
"I was by his side, a master crafter, delighting him day by
day, ever at play in his presence, at play everywhere in the
world, delighting to be with the children of humanity"
(Book of Wisdom 8:30-31).

Another insight that Vaillant's research uncovered
was the shape of the resource of generativity: both care
as a person reaching outward to contribute to the world,
whether with family or career, and interiority, turning
inward to listen to new concerns of the heart. "At age
forty—give or take as much as a decade—men leave the
compulsive, unreflective busy work of their occupational
apprenticeship and once more become explorers of the
world within."

For some of the men Vaillant was following, midlife
meant a change in vocation. Invitations to leadership
emerged, and they assumed tasks they were not trained
for. "Being truly responsible for others is no job for the
specialist."

Daniel Levinson's book *The Seasons of a Man's Life*
focused on adult maturing in midlife through the metaphor of "a dream." At the beginning of our adult years our
life ambition arises like a dream: to be a doctor or journalist or astronaut. At this point one's dream is often bigger
than life as its energy stretches us with large ambitions.
In our forties we have a chance to revisit the dream. Has
it withered and been lost along the way? Does it demand

a course correction? Has it been lived out obsessively, crowding out other plans and hopes?

Levinson argued that the dream/vocation in midlife may need to undergo what he called a "de-illusionment." The dream often begins with some illusions: high-flown visions of what we might accomplish. The challenge is not one of "disillusionment" but to let go some of the more illusory dreams of youth, allowing the dream to better fit my life as it is now at forty or fifty. We could also call this a reconciliation of the dream. For some this is the recognition that I have fulfilled my parents' dream (the doctor or priest they always wanted); now I must turn to a life-ambition that is more genuinely mine. For some women they turn their energies from family care to a career outside the home. Or it may be a realization that I have accomplished the dream and new vistas await.

During this decade of the 1970s we were blessed with colleagues like James Zullo and Gordon Myers, who challenged and advanced our own thinking about adult religious maturing. In 1978 we took a leave from Notre Dame and wrote our first book *Christian Life Patterns: The Psychological Challenges and Religious Invitations of Adult Life.* Bringing these ideas to a first fruition was deeply satisfying and we resolved not to return to Notre Dame. Our own vocation was leading us beyond academia, and instead we began lecturing at dioceses and religious congregations on topics of adult faith. The next stage of our own vocation was taking shape.

Chapter Two

Finding Our Vocation: Notre Dame and Pastoral Theology

*The sense of the faithful: "to cling to the faith once deliv-
ered to the Saints, penetrate it more deeply by accurate
insights, and apply it more thoroughly to life."* (Vatican
II, "Light to the Nations")

In 1973 we arrived at Notre Dame with the charge of
refashioning the moribund program of field education.
"Field Education" had only just been conceived as an
effort to immerse seminarians in the practical life of faith.
In addition to their courses in theology—Scripture, ethics, history—the seminarians might leave academia for
an hour or two and go into "the field," visiting pastoral
settings such as a vibrant parish, or hospital chaplaincy,
even a prison where they might bring their more academic study into contact with the ground-level experience
of faith. (This last example, we found, could be hazard-
ous to one's faith. The seminarian might notice that the
majority of prisoners were Black; he might become newly
aware of the death penalty and the commandment to not
kill—unsettling questions that could disturb one's faith.)

Why were we as a recently married couple hired
to direct seminarians in their faith? I had been a Jesuit

seminarian, then taught seminarians in a college in South Korea for three years before returning to the United States for more studies in theology prior to leaving the Jesuits to marry Evelyn. One could say that a decade in the seminary in two different countries made me a professional seminarian.

As directors of field education we would help our students reflect on what they were learning. The hope was for seminarians to begin to see themselves as capable of theological reflection, of relating the theology they were learning in the classroom to the everyday practice of faith. At this time the seminary at Notre Dame was undergoing post-Vatican II experiments: lay women and men were allowed, for the first time, to study alongside priesthood candidates. This itself would demand reflection: what was lay ministry? We were answering this question for ourselves as we continued to teach at Loyola in the summer time.

In 1976, Father Robert Pelton, CSC, initiated a program of priestly renewal at the university. In a sabbatical movement that would soon become widespread in the U.S. church, priests would bring their several decades of experience in ministry to Notre Dame with the goal of reflecting on the strengths and shortcomings of their own ministry. There would be the opportunity to learn of new currents in theology as well as space to reflect on more personal and practical issues. For this, Father Pelton would need to recruit faculty who could combine academic instruction with the opportunity for such practical reflection.

For Father Pelton's program Evelyn and I began to construct lectures that would do just that: combine academic input along with the opportunity for participants to reflect on their experience. How, for example, did their experience of priesthood differ from what they had learned in the seminary several decades earlier? Questions about community leadership might be juxtaposed with a discussion of their particular parish. Instead of fifty-minute lectures, we would speak for a half hour and then invite participants to ask themselves pointed questions about the relevance of this material. Where did they meet a pastoral question—of personal crisis as a spiritual opportunity, or the collaboration of clergy and laity, or tensions between women and men? In such reflections we were constantly confronting the question of personal experience and its influence on their lives as priests.

Two very similar programs arose at Notre Dame during these same years. Monsignor Jack Egan, exiled from his own diocese of Chicago, began a program for women religious, especially those in transition from leadership. Father Vince Dwyer arrived at the university to create another sabbatical program for priests. Then in the late 1970s, the theology department initiated a PhD program in pastoral theology. The pastoral focus of this program was greeted with suspicion by the more academically oriented faculty and after only three years the program was allowed to die.

Theological Reflection

During these same years Catholic scholars were becoming newly focused on the question of theological reflection: how to think about the faith and its expression in a post–Vatican II church? A mood of change, of *aggiornamento* (updating), prevailed in those years. The bishops at the

Council had decided to change the language of the liturgy from traditional Latin to the vernacular of each culture. What reflections had led them to this significant decision? Theologian David Tracy, in *Blessed Rage for Order* (1975), had begun to speak of such reflection as a correlation of "common human experience" and "the Christian fact." At first this raised its own questions: is there such a thing as a shared "common human experience" and what exactly does "correlation" mean?

Meanwhile, theologian Bernard Lonergan, in his *Method in Theology* (1972), had launched an elaborate schema of how theological reflection might proceed while honoring the many differing aspects of history and philosophy. As I recall, his method had eight core elements. It was intricate and complex, but how could it guide a practical reflection among ministers about some question of faith?

Two metaphors rose to prominence in these discussions: theological reflection as "a conversation" between faith and culture: the sacred tradition of Scripture speaks to the present cultural moment, which in turn questions this ancient heritage. Where in such a dialogue did personal experience arise and what was its authority?

The metaphor of conversation was fraught with other concerns: can one question our sacred heritage or our Scripture? A conversation usually implies some equality among discussants, but how can the enormous authority of the Christian tradition and our own fragile lives enter a genuine conversation? Here arose a central question that still challenges today: what is personal experience worth? How does the unique experience of this person or that community dare raise its voice in dialogue with a sacred heritage?

Our colleague in the theology department, the biblical scholar Eugene Ulrich, helped the participants in our discussions recognize how some religious experience is remembered and retold again and again. Eventually the experience—of a brilliant bush that looked like it was on fire or survival in a hostile desert—itself becomes the tradition.

The second metaphor was that of "befriending." Reflecting on the Catholic tradition, one confronted a massive and authoritative source of information. How to become more comfortable with this heritage? We remembered that this heritage was both divine and human: it was made up of revelation but also the misinterpretations and malpractice that are necessarily a part of any religious history. Assessing the contemporary culture, we were aware that God dwells here too; how to discern "the signs of the times" taking place in one's culture? Befriending one's own experience could be even more intimidating. What is my modest experience worth? How can I bring it into dialogue with my faith and my culture?

Practical, Portable, and Communal

We soon learned that the intricacy of Lonergan's method placed it well beyond the skill level of our students, and our own. Tracy's method was more manageable and suggested the path that we eventually took. We came to see that theological reflection includes both a model and a method. The model names the three conversation partners of religious heritage (the Christian faith), the surrounding culture, and the experience of this specific community or individual. The method speaks to the dynamic that moves the model: how to question these three sources of information in the direction of some pastoral, practical decision.

The goal was not a theoretical one, but practical: what action should this pastor or this community make to render the faith more accessible to their community? And the method should be portable; a flexible style of reflection that one could bring from the seminary to different pastoral contexts where the priest or lay minister finds herself. And finally the method should be communal: a style of refection that a group could use to think about its own life.

The goal here was replacing the lone-ranger model of the pastor simply making all decisions in a community of faith. In the post-Vatican II church communities were experimenting with parish councils. What was such a group to do? What was the best style of interaction?

Aware of the practical aspect of such reflection we struggled to include the notion of "skills" in the discussion. Listening respectfully to others is not a casual event, but a discipline. This does not happen automatically; nor is it a matter of a pastor responding, "I understand exactly how you feel." Scholars such as Gerard Egan at Loyola University, in his influential *The Skilled Helper,* were outlining what this skill entailed, as well as those of confrontation and conflict resolution. These were skills of leadership but were not taught in seminaries at that time. (Our own efforts to install a skills sequence in the seminary curriculum failed; we were told that newly ordained priests "just pick up these skills.")

In 1975 we received a grant from the Lilly Foundation for a two-year-long reflection with persons actively engaged in ministry—four women and four priests—and four faculty. The research led to the publication of our book *Method in Ministry*. Many of the theologians in the department showed little interest in it, while pastors and other ministers seemed grateful for some guidance in how to reflect theologically.

What Is Pastoral Theology?

During these years of teaching at the University of Notre Dame we were all becoming attuned to a new discipline in theology. Something called pastoral theology. The theological reflection that we were exploring came to be the core dynamic of this new discipline. Protestant theologians had been at this well before Catholics. Seward Hiltner, in *Preface to Pastoral Theology* (1958), stressed ministry—"shepherding"—as the proper focus of pastoral theology. That is, not the question of doctrine but the practice of the faith. How is Christian faith expressed or "practiced"? Method suddenly became important; a pastoral theologian should be able to explain what she was doing.

From quite another direction, Anton Boisen, after episodes in his own life of mental illness, created a program of training ministers called Clinical Pastoral Education (CPE). Seminary students, after spending some time in a hospital setting, would select one "critical incident," report on it, and have it critiqued by a peer group. Boisen had learned the hard way that life experience and especially suffering must be part of a minister's education. Running through this emerging discipline was the question: what sense do Christian beliefs make in the face of suffering? Herb Anderson has expressed this orientation well in pointing to the partnership of pastoral theology with psychology and his phrasing: "person- and pathos-centered."

Meanwhile, the Catholic Church lacked the "academic infrastructure" to support anything like pastoral theology. (We were heirs of that lack.) David Tracy led many others in the effort to cobble together strategies and methods for thinking about these implications for Catholic faith in the modern world. During our years at the University of Notre Dame we learned by doing pastoral theology. And in the doing we came into our vocation as pastoral theologians.

Pastoral Theology and
a Meditation on Time

Be careful then how you live ... redeem the time.
(Ephesians 5:16)

Pastoral theology, in its infancy, had to struggle against the general persuasion that it consisted mainly of applying theological ideas to the life of faith. Theological reflection looked like a one-way street. Could pastoral theology become a more active partner in theological reflection? We chose as a test case the question of time.

In our interactions with seminarians at Notre Dame we became aware that they, like many other graduate students, often felt stressed out by all the academic demands on their time. There seemed to never be enough time. Class after class brought ideas that, however enlightening, could not be fully savored and integrated into their lives of ministry. Time itself never came under review. The twenty-four-hour day simple enveloped them with all its constraints.

We invited students to recall how our Christian heritage was filled with ideas about time itself. The very idea of a Sabbath as a time-out suggested that time was malleable. We could alter how we spend our time, punctuating a week of labor with a respite that God had insisted on. (Of course, ministers work on the Sabbath; this just reinforced the question of how to deal with the time of our lives.)

The ebb and flow of our days are susceptible to boredom or compulsion as well as epiphanies of beauty and grace. Christians have long sought creative ways to bend time to their own purposes: the weeks of Advent and Lent's forty days shaped the liturgical year. Then there was the cosmology that once reigned: a creation only a few thousand years old with an apocalyptic end looming. "Christian time" has long been shaped by "the four last things"—death, judgment, heaven or hell. We are rightfully apprehensive about an ending filled with threat.

In recent years a more cosmically apt image began to emerge: billions of years of an unfolding creation, overseen by a Creator who is comfortable with such vastness. Romano Guardini wrote of a "God of patience" who "allows things to develop at their own pace waiting until the time is ripe" (*Jubilee*, May 1957, 19). What a shift from the previously harried image in the poem "The Hound of Heaven" of God pursuing souls "down the nights and down the days, down the labyrinthan ways of (one's) own mind."

We also invited the students to recall two very different words for time in the Scriptures. The Greek word *chronos* (as in chronic) appears when Jesus is asked to heal a sick person. "How long a time (*chronos*) has this person been ill?" (Mark 9:2). Time as *chronos* also points to periods when a person is bored or is possessed by some obsession: too much time or never enough time.

In other contexts the New Testament uses the word *kairos* to describe a very different experience of time. Mark's Gospel announces that the beginning of Jesus's public life signals that "the time *(kairos)* has come" (1:15). A special time, time to wake up, get involved, or time to change the course of one's life. It is the time for the harvest or to give birth. In Psalm 71 the psalmist prays, "do not abandon me in the *kairos* of my old age."

In pastoral theology the language of Scripture invites us to ask questions about forces in our lives. Many experience time today as driven by demands seeded into our culture (think of FOMO—fear of missing out). Do we even have choices about how we spend our time? Such questions lie at the heart of a spirituality of time that will give the future priest and lay minister a more centered life.

The Winter of Our Content

Leaving Notre Dame? It isn't done. Yet as we glanced around during our years in the theology department we became aware that we were appreciated but had few genuine colleagues. When the pastoral theology specialty was closed down we realized it was time to move on.

At that time we were receiving more invitations from dioceses and parishes to help their staffs reflect theologically together. Perhaps this was our path that would take us beyond the constraints of academia directly into questions of how to practice pastoral theology.

In January 1978 we took an unpaid leave from the university and subletting a house on the shores of Lake

Michigan set out to write a book we would call *Christian Life Patterns*. As it turned out we had chosen one of the Midwest's worst winters (twenty-nine inches of snow in one late January blizzard), but we were content. Together we wrote in the morning and, bundling up, went on walks in the afternoon. In four months the book was done, and a decision had been made not to return to the university.

Over the next years we were finding the shape of our own vocation serving the church beyond the academy. We continued to be tethered to Loyola in Chicago, teaching there in the summers and giving an occasional workshop during the year. We gave ourselves the only slightly pretentious name Whitehead Associates as we built our own style of theological reflection.

CHAPTER THREE

Learning to Play Together: Scarcity and Abundance

Stoic philosopher Marcus Aurelius: "The art of living is more about wrestling than dancing." I agreed until my wife taught me how to dance.

In the 1950s Catholics stayed in their lanes. Priests provided leadership, and lay Catholics, too often, were content with the cliché of pray, pay, and obey.

In the 1960s and '70s this began to change. Catholics were becoming engaged in parish councils. Groups like Marriage Encounter and Christ Renews His Parish were flourishing. Catholic hospitals welcomed more lay chaplains as the number of sisters and priests continued to diminish. Other experiments in lay ministry were growing, questioning the traditional "lone-ranger" model of a single priestly leader burdened with all the decision-making chores within a community of faith.

As Catholics struggled to learn the skills of cooperation and collaboration, they were challenged to hold each other in new embraces. In the past they may have held their priest leader in great esteem, but not friendship. The metaphors of Marcus Aurelius came into view: wrestling in conflict and dancing with affection. Did these have a place in a community of faith?

The metaphor of holding embraces a wide range of relationships. We hold close friends in an embrace of affection. We hold our children accountable. At times we hold each other in conflict, wrestling toward a new embrace. We may have grown up in a family where we were held back, not encouraged to express ourselves. Or even held down; girls don't serve at the altar. The kiss of peace, restored to the liturgy, invited uncomfortable embraces. Many men had learned to hold themselves slightly aloof, cautious about too intimate sharing. A name for this is composure. Composure begins as self-possession, a style of "self-holding" and "self-protecting." But composure may begin to look like aloofness, a stand-offishness that begins to look like an absence of neediness. Then self-holding becomes self-hiding, insulating a person from threatening contact with others.

If we are fortunate, loved ones succeed in whittling away at this composure. "You lose the world that you hoped vainly to control, the world in which you would be invulnerable to hurt, misfortune, and loss of identity, and you regain it as the world that the mind and will can grasp because they have stopped trying to hold it still or to hold it away" (Roberto Unger).

"A Discipleship of Equals"

The Vatican Council had shifted the focus of ministry from the sacrament of priestly Ordination to the sacrament of Baptism. Now we realized that all are called and gifted to serve, in a variety of ways, the needs and hopes of the community. Now it was possible to envision the faith community as "a discipleship of equals" and ministry "as the responsibility of all and the charge of some."

The Council had also returned to the ancient ideal of "a sense of the faithful" (*sensus fidelium*), a picture of faith as a communal conviction of how to express our faith in this time and this place (*Lumen Gentium,* #12). Cardinal Newman, a century and a half ago, had defined this communal conviction as "an instinct in the body of Christ." To arrive at such a consensus demands considerable skills of collaboration.

During the decade of the 1980s Evelyn and I began to offer workshops for groups that were seeking to implement this sense of the faithful in their own communities. We were invited to various dioceses to assist in the building of a more collaborative ministry. Educators like the Christian Brothers also invited us to explore with them the gifts and challenges of collaboration in their schools. For both of these groups the specific challenge was to equip a new generation of lay leaders who would carry on the charism, or special calling, of these groups.

Partners, Not Parents

Throughout the church there seemed to be a growing conviction that ministry involved an adult partnership rather than a parenting of the children of God. At issue, of course, was the deep tradition of a hierarchical vision of the church. This vertical vision of the church was captured in a single phrase of St. Augustine that was quoted in the Council: "from the bishops down to the last lay person." Not just the downward descent but the very last lay person. Who might this be?

In the ancient tradition of the church we had long cherished a paternalistic vision of the leadership of the priest as "father" while we spoke of the pope as "papa." The community of faith was composed of "the children of God." If these images have a certain charm—the warmth and protection of parental leaders—they can end as infantilizing adult believers, encouraging them to a passivity that is more fitting for children than adult Christians.

A developmental vision of how Christians mature can help to see through the limits of a hierarchical model of ministry. We are, all of us, children of God; this relationship never ends. And at the same time, we grow into an adult expression of our faith. This means taking ourselves seriously, attentive to gifts that God has given us, and a willingness to contribute to the faith community where we find ourselves. Adult faith is described in the language of discipleship when as adult followers we invest ourselves in the virtues and responsibility of adults. And the journey does not end here. As we continue to mature as parents and teachers, some of us are called to leadership roles, whether this is initiating an outreach to the poor in our neighborhood or heading up the parish council. Disciples, in the Gospels and in our experience, mature into stewards, those with some leadership role in the community. The challenge is to remember that even stewards—whether bishops, or priestly pastors, or the lay head of the parish council—also remain children of God.

Obeying as Adults

Obeying as adults differs from this virtue in children. Here obedience consists in a commitment to one another. No longer a matter of doing what we are told ("because I said so"); now obedience is listening with respect, paying attention. The Greek term for obedience in the New Testament is *akouein*—"to listen." The word survives in the English term acoustics. Obedience becomes a pleasure when the acoustics in a community is good. We hear one another well; there is no static or interference in the air.

After Vatican II, a new vocabulary arose: discernment that arises as individuals and groups listening to the Spirit as they chart their way forward. Unfortunately the church suffered a disastrous experiment in an early effort to listen and discern. Married couples were included in a church-wide effort to discern whether birth control was not unnatural—as it had long seemed to its unmarried clergy—but in fact aided couples in the management of their families. But the pope, under pressure from conservative leaders, chose not to trust this discernment and decreed that birth control was not for Catholics. One could say he disobeyed the emerging consensus of the wider community, the sense of the faithful.

The Enigma of Scarcity and Abundance

A large crowd has come to listen to Jesus. The day is late and they are in a deserted spot—a scarcity of both time and resources. When Jesus tells his friends to feed the people, they complain that they have only a few loaves of bread and some fish. Jesus tells them to go through crowd and gather what they could find. When they return, Jesus blessed these resources; and the food is distributed, and—amazingly—there turns out to be more than enough to feed the entire group. "All ate and were filled. What was left over was gathered up, twelve baskets of broken pieces" (Luke 9:19).

This is a parable of scarcity and abundance: an abundance of people are fed despite a seeming scarcity of resources. Was this a one-time event, a miracle that only Jesus, the son of God, could accomplish? Or is there, perhaps, a larger message here: resources held in private and kept out of circulation will always mean a scarcity in the larger community. Jesus turns fragmented resources and privately held sustenance into bountiful nourishment. By sharing their meager amount of food the people seem to multiply it; breaking their bread, they made more of it. Apparent scarcity often obscures a hidden abundance.

"I have come so they may have life and have it in abundance" (John 10:10). The Gospels recount again and again the interplay of scarcity and abundance. The core account of Jesus's message of abundance—his feeding the multitudes—appears five times in the Synoptic Gospels. The story itself is multiplied, emphasizing the point of abundance.

Generous Absence in Three Parts

A beloved pastor in a thriving parish is taken sick. He is forced to step aside from his usual leadership role. Three women who had been assisting him are suddenly thrust into decision-making roles. They might panic; we are not up this. We are only faithful disciples following the guidance of our parish steward. Then a curious thing often happens. They discover they are more talented than they thought. In the leader's absence they step into his role and find they have the skills (and soon the confidence) to do many of his leadership tasks. The unintended absence of a traditional leader generates new gifts and emerging skills.

Jesus's disciples had gathered in an upper room, a space where he was conspicuously absent. When they wondered what to do next, they were only looking at one another. Their reliance on Jesus was not available now. Then in this distressing vacuum they felt some stirring of wind, some force entering this emptiness. Suddenly they felt confident in preaching what Jesus had taught them. Jesus's absence in that room had created space for the Spirit to move. It was a generous absence.

British psychologist D. W. Winnicott performed experiments with parents and their young children who were given toys to absorb their attention. Meanwhile the parent withdrew to the opposite corner of the room. Without the dominant presence of the parent the child began to concentrate and play with a new attention. He was "alone in the presence of another." The other was very much present, as one commentator noted, "to cover the risk" (if some emergency arose) but in an unobtrusive way.

The Invention of Scarcity

Scarcity, of course, is often genuine: the poverty that afflicts so much of the world; the enduring lack of strength that accompanies a long illness; our inability to solve problems in our own family. Scarcity can be very real and most painful. Often, however, scarcity is more apparent than real. Another town lacks food, and our storerooms are full. Or becoming depressed, we are convinced that we have no friends, while these very persons gather at our gate, waiting to be re-admitted to our life. Scarcity may be not only apparent but fabricated: a human invention and a social practice. The expensive watch retains its value only if it remains scarce; the status associated with a luxury automobile is diminished if too many people obtain one. Consumerism trains us in an economy of necessary scarcity.

The church, led by fallible humans, falls prey to the temptation to create scarcity. When the church decides that lay persons cannot preach at a Eucharistic service, it depreciates these gifts and manufactures scarcity. When liturgical leadership is restricted to unmarried men, we all but guarantee that the sacraments will be in short supply. This fabrication of scarcity reached its apex in the historical declaration that "there is no salvation outside the church." The church now has the franchise on salvation, ensuring it will be made scarce.

But Christians, in their better moments, recognize the gifts that flourish among them. Taking advantage of these charisms and talents, a community of faith recovers a God-given abundance. In Jesus Christ, God has given us great abundance. We, the church, continue to invent scarcity. And yet clues and hints abound in this world of scarcity of God's abundant, even extravagant gifts.

Speaking of Extravagance

These days we are all being educated in a cosmic extravagance: a creation forming over billions of years; many millions of galaxies; hundreds of species of ants. What is such abundance about if not the inclination of the Creator to excess?

Yet another economy runs through the Christian Scriptures. This one, no surprise, mimics the economy of the world we know well. Everyone should pay his own way;

"You reap what you sow" (Galatians 6:7). And yet more dramatically, the right of payback: "an eye for an eye, a tooth for a tooth" (Exodus 21:24).

But, in fact, we do not reap what we sow. We reap what others before us have sown. We inherit what our ancestors have done, arriving late on the scene and already in debt. An economy of excess plays through the story of the prodigal son. Returning home he may have expected the worst but receives instead the extravagant affection of his father. Another son objects but to no avail.

When Jesus speaks of the exchange of giving and receiving we expect one thing and hear something quite different. "Give and it will be given to you," says Jesus, then adds, "a good measure, pressed down, shaken together, running over, will be put in your lap" (Luke 6:38). You will not receive your due but something more, so much that it overflows the little vessel of your heart.

Paul uses a single Greek term—*perisseuein*—for God's extravagance, but the English text must resort to three different words: in his letter to those in Ephesus he writes of the grace that God "has lavished" on them (1:8); to those in Philippia, he encourages them to let their love "overflow" (1:9); and in the First Letter to the Thessalonians he prays that God may cause their love "to abound" (3:12).

Retrenchment

As the decade of the 1980s came to a close, the enthusiasm for collaborative ministry began to wane. A retrenchment in the broader church was afoot. Pope John Paul II and many bishops were emphasizing the distinctive place of the priest. He was not one of many ministers collaborating in the community but uniquely called to a vocation that sets him apart. Dioceses were turning to an earlier notion of the priest as the one sacred minister whom others assisted. The Vatican II dream of ministry as "the responsibility of all and the charge of some" was being eroded.

We observed this entrenchment in our own ministry. Planners for a diocese invited us to lead a discussion of collaboration in ministry in a gathering that would include only priests. When we suggested that collaboration begins with the idea of cooperation among the many members of a community, the planners said they were concerned that if lay persons attended, fewer priests would come. We gradually convinced the planners to include the most engaged lay leaders in the diocese. Their compromise: the lay leaders could listen to the lecture but were expected to leave the room before the discussion. (They declined to leave.)

In a workshop in a large parish, the recently arrived pastor complained that the woman religious who had worked in the community for many years was not a good collaborator. The reason: "she doesn't do what I tell her."

The church was returning to the tradition vision of the priest as uniquely endowed with the gifts of leadership, thus the chief minister of a parish or other group. He might be encouraged to delegate authority, but power lies first and last with him.

Conclusion

During the 1980s and beyond, collaboration at Loyola remained alive. We often co-taught a course or workshop. Evelyn and I wrote essays with our colleagues. We found ourselves assisting groups that were crafting new styles of collaboration: parishes, hospitals, religious congregations.

Our most precious collaboration were yearly gatherings with Bernard Lee and Michael Cowan. The four of us shared early drafts of essays, complemented by Bernard's cassoulet. This delightful exchange continued for nearly forty years, "until death do us part."

We learned as we went, sometime encouraged, sometime dismayed, by old, unmovable patterns of power and authority. It was often, of course, a strain: deadlines suffered and disagreements flourished. But the gain outperformed the strain. As the larger church geared down, we and our colleagues continued to lift up the abundance of gifts sprouting all around. From these conversations grew a book on collaborative ministry we entitled *The Promise of Partnership* (1991).

Evelyn and Jim between lectures in Sydney, Australia

Part Two

Fruitful Embraces

CHAPTER FOUR

Speaking of Sexuality—
The 1980s

A woman came to him with an alabaster jar of very costly ointment and she poured it over his head as he sat at table. (Matthew 26:6)

When we married in 1970 we assumed that sexuality was a private matter. It was not something that people discuss in polite company. Our sexual lives were nobody else's business. God, as it turned out, had other plans. In our first years of teaching, both at Loyola and Notre Dame, students regularly came to us, wanting to talk about their sexual concerns and hopes. Why us? This is the kind of question that God has yet to answer.

Through the 1970s we listened to these young generous Catholics who were so eager to fathom the movements of their sexual selves and find a greater comfort with their bodies. They recognized their bodies as both blessed and broken. This eagerness led to their longing to talk more openly about their sexuality, whether they were married or single.

As the 1970s turned into the 1980s, we began offering workshops, often a two-day event, on sexuality. We were

not attempting to provide solutions to common puzzle-
ments about our sexual lives, but to expand the discussion,
trusting that participants were already edging toward a
richer appreciation of sexuality. All of us were seeking to
reclaim the optimism at the heart of the Incarnation: God
made flesh. As our colleague Dick Westley observed, "It is
time for sexually active believers to proclaim in the Lord's
name, and without fear, what they have learned in bed,
confident that it is . . . as authoritative as any episcopal letter or papal encyclical."

Speaking of sexuality: where to begin? Not with hot-
button issues such as abortion or premarital sexual intercourse. Instead, to begin with two dynamics at the heart
of human life: the sensual pleasure of touch and the challenges of genuine intimacy.

The church often softens the story of the woman pouring oil over Jesus's head by interpreting it as an anointing
before his coming death. This symbolic interpretation is
likely to deflect our appreciation of the pleasure of the oil
itself. Because we are uncomfortable with sensuality?

Sexuality names the energy that quickens, delights,
and makes us most fully human. Even at the beginning of
things we face a puzzlement: "The paradox of sexuality .
. . is that it both links us with other people and makes us
feel at odds with ourselves" (Adam Philips).

Moral theologian Steven Pope writes, "The Church
stands as the most visibly identifiable moral voice in the
Western world. It offers a profound core of moral wisdom regarding sex, marriage, and the family that is badly
needed by societies in which people feel increasingly iso-
lated, objectified and bereft of moral substance." But "the
content and tone of its own statements have exacerbated

matters by reinforcing the view of some observers that its sexual ethics is simply out of touch with contemporary experience."

Sensuality and Intimacy

Sexuality, it turns out, is about so much more than sex. It is about the power of sensual touch. I remember Evelyn describing for our class the experience that many women have of putting on a favorite silk blouse, saved for special occasions. The sheer pleasure of the silk against their skin.

Then there is the sensual pleasure of a hot bath as water blesses a tired and distracted body, which, in turn, surrenders to the ministry of the water. And the pleasure of a meal taken with loved ones, the sensuality of taste enhancing the bond that binds us ever deeper together. "Taste and see the goodness of the Lord" (Psalm 34:8). Theologian Bernard Lee comments: "It is God's intention for people to enjoy the earth and its abundance. . . . In tasting how sweet the succulent food and fine strained wines are, one can also taste and experience how sweet is God."

And here we have to mention another kind of touch that is a direct ministry to the flesh. Mary Ann Finch directs a program called "Healing Through Touch" in the Tenderloin area of San Francisco. This is a service at one of her pop-up centers where trained volunteers offer massage to people of the street, often the homeless. Here you see volunteers pressing skilled hands deep into tired shoulders and necks or, even more dramatically, massaging the feet of these people on the move. This touching, oddly intimate and humbling at once, recalls the anointing of feet at the liturgy of Holy Thursday.

In "Touch in the Death Chamber," Sister Helen Prejean advocates for healing touch even for a prisoner about to be executed by the state (*New York Times,* Sunday, November 14, 2021, p. 7); she recalls being allowed to hold a man near the moment of execution. Touching him she kept saying, "Look at my face. I will be the face of Christ." After the execution she went outside and threw up.

Is the church "out of touch"? Many Christians have learned not to trust touch, but a growing comfort with sensual touch prepares us for the hesitant, thrilling touch of the lover and reminds us that such touch is all respect and responsiveness and not about domination. Saint Paul reminds us that salvation itself is a matter of "God's good pleasure." Do not forget, "It is God who is at work in you, enabling you both to will and work for God's good pleasure" (Philippians 2:13).

If sexuality is about sensuality, it is also about intimacy. Participants in our classes would often wondered, "What is intimacy? Do you mean having sex?" Intimacy names the capacity to draw close to another in daring and trusting ways. It is the ability to trust ourselves with our own feelings of sensuality as well as trust ourselves into another's embrace.

Intimacy refers to the many ways we hold one another. But this capacity begins at home: comfort with myself, this particular body with its hungers and hesitations. Self-intimacy is the developing comfort with this embodied self; this is, after all, what we bring to another in friendship and affection. The psychological capacity for intimacy is at the heart of friendship. It is the willingness to draw close without being overwhelmed or needing to seize control. Intimacy is forged in multiple embraces. We hold one another in collaboration at work; we hold our children, and ourselves, accountable. We may have learned not to risk such encounters, to hold others at arm's length. We cannot risk the dangers of genuine friendship. If we are fortunate we learn that intimacy is not optional.

The psychologist Erik Erikson has described the components of this capacity: to commit ourselves to particular people, in relationships that last over time, and meet the accompanying demands for change in ways that do not compromise personal integrity. As a youth we may have loved "humanity" but could not abide all those imperfect others. We may also have learned to avoid "particular friendships." Then we learned that is the only kind of friendship there is. In every lasting friendship and in the bonds of committed love we meet another arena of intimacy: holding one another in conflict. Would that it were not so. With youthful ideals of romance we might believe that affection knows no conflict and only over time are we challenged to embrace this aspect of a maturing relationship.

The Desire to Be Fruitful

Sexuality sponsors new life. Sometimes with a child; often with other forms of fruitfulness. The experience of love-making enriches the couple's affection and deepens their mutual commitment; these are expressions of fruitfulness. A great calamity for the Catholic Church has been its shrinking fruitfulness into reproduction. Believing that sexual intercourse, with its powerful arousals, was a near occasion of sin, the church has often taught that sexual pleasure could be forgiven if it engenders a child. Fruitfulness beyond reproduction received little attention.

A painful crisis arose after Vatican II when married lay persons—for the first time—were queried about birth control. Their vote for responsible managing of births was overturned in the decision that in the summer of 1968 produced the papal teaching of *Humanae Vitae*.

Fruitfulness remains as a central concern of marriage. Our own fifty years together seem, to us, fruitful in teaching and writing. The absence of children does not appear as a blight. In fact, this aspect of our marriage has opened us to an awareness of the committed fruitfulness of gay and lesbian lives. All this began at both Loyola and Notre Dame as young gay and lesbians sought us out in an effort to fathom the wretched judgment that the Catholic Church had made on them. These were young Catholics loving the church but being told, in response, that the direction of their affection was "objectively disordered."

At Notre Dame the students were seminarians preparing for a priestly vocation, yet they were being told that their every stirring of delight in regard to another male was sordid and unnatural. They knew priests in their congregation who were gay, but there seemed to be some code of secrecy about this. None of this was promising for their own vocation.

At Loyola we remember a conversation with a person in the summer program who had become attracted to another participant. They had recently taken the "L" to Lincoln Park and just walked around, hand in hand. It was this "hand in hand" that triggered in Evelyn and myself the recognition of the similarity of attraction. What he was feeling was what we had felt and still did; this was the same ignition of delight, the same blessed chemistry that lies at the heart of all creation. The church had it wrong when it insisted that such stirrings were unnatural.

We made an early response to this question in a 1987 essay on "The Shape of Compassion: Reflections on Catholics and Homosexuality" (*Spirituality Today*): "A deep wound in the body of Christ has been opened once again. The wound is the ancient suspicion of sexuality that continues to infect Christian life."

We wrote that the limitations of this narrow, philosophical view of marital fruitfulness were becoming obvious. It makes of sex both "too much" and "too little." It places too much emphasis on particular sexual activities, while failing to appreciate the larger contribution to a shared life. Such an approach constrains sexuality to narrow biological purposes and neglects the delightful range of these arousals. Such an attitude defeats the church's own ideals of an incarnational faith.

Closets: Safe but Darkly Confining

Several generations ago many homosexuals learned that the safest place to exist was in a closet: out of sight, if in the dark. Not calling attention to oneself. It was a confining area but seemingly secure. In time we have all learned that this is not a natural habitat for humans, not a place to live and grow.

Andrew Sullivan has written of his efforts to stay out of sight. He tried to keep his relationships superficial "to avoid passion breaking out." What resulted was "a theological austerity that became the essential complement to an emotional emptiness." What resulted was "a lie covered over by a career."

Happily this unhealthy state did not endure. He remembers "the exhilaration as I felt my sexuality began to be incorporated into my life . . . a sense of being suffused at last with the possibility of being fully myself before those I loved and before God."

Devoted sexual loving is more than "a remedy for concupiscence" (Augustine). It is, with its unexpected and unearned delights, an echo of creation. Sexual sharing can be not a near occasion of sin, but a near occasion of grace.

We began to see that being gay or lesbian was not a choice; instead it was "a bestowed identity," in the words of Episcopal bishop Bennet Sims. We were reminded that "sexual orientation embraces more than the object of erotic passion. It involves our desire for the goods of intimacy, friendship and romantic relationships" (theologian Jack Bonsor). We began paying attention to what the human sciences were saying. In 1973 the American Psychiatric Association removed homosexuality from its list of mental disorders, and two years later the American Psychological Association followed suit. What did they know that still eluded church leaders?

In the course of many conversations with gay and lesbian Catholics we have experienced, again and again, a conversion of empathy. What if homosexuals (should we retire that term that so blatantly over-emphasizes a person's sexuality?) are not "them," dangerously different people whose lives are consumed in deviant behavior? What if the truth is much simpler and more significant: we are the Body of Christ and part of this body is lesbian and gay?

These members of the Body are our siblings and children, our friends and fellow parishioners. These are persons like the rest of us striving to live generous lives of maturing faith. As we speak the truth to one another, we recognize that, in our sexuality as in so much else, we are more alike than different. This realization marks the beginning of a church healing itself.

CHAPTER FIVE

Living with Passion

*There are some revelations into our own and other peo-
ple's humanity that we achieve only through experiences
of passion.* (Roberto Unger)

To be human is to be aroused. Emotion ignites our best
behaviors: courage in the face of danger, a fierce attach-
ment to our children, the anger that resists injustice. Our
emotions also impel us to our worst excesses: violent rage,
sexual abuse, corrosive guilt. Even though we can hardly
live with our distressing feelings, we cannot live without
them. In their absence we may survive for awhile, but we
will not thrive.

In the enthusiasm for collaboration that marked the
1980s many of us were being challenged to learn new
ways to be in touch with one another. An earlier piety
had encouraged us to hold others at a safe distance. Any
embrace more intimate seemed beyond our vocation.

But the up-close challenges of collaboration—questioning, disagreeing, compromising—led us to a new
interest in the messy business of emotions and the passions. We began assessing passions such as anger, shame,

and loneliness as not simply threatening but as bearing important information about our life with others and with God.

At first the cards seemed stacked against such up-close attention to emotions. The Enlightenment in the eighteenth century had endorsed reason as the one path to level-headed interaction. The great philosopher Kant judged that emotions are "probably always an illness of mind because both emotion and passion exclude the sovereignty of reason . . .emotions make one more or less blind."

Ambiguity about the passions had run deep in the Christian heritage. Augustine was suspicious of the vehemence of passion, especially sexual passion and its threat to the ideal of self-control. Aquinas, eight centuries later, reversed course, seeing the passions as the very vitality that fuels our virtues as well as our vices. Anger may often be sinful, but there is a force called just anger that marshals our energy to confront injustice. Shame may register a crippling sense of inferiority, but a healthy sense of shame anchors our self-respect. "Have you no sense of shame?" The passions may disrupt our life, but they also energize us to live more fully.

During the decade of the 1980s, scholars had begun to recognize that the powerful emotions we call passions are cognitive: more than hormonal surges they are, indeed, honorable parts of our reasoning. Roberto Unger reminded us of the limits of reason. "Reason gives us knowledge of the world, but it cannot tell us in the final instance what to want or what to do." And reason suffers other deficits; it "cannot provide the quality of sustained commitment that we need to pursue our most reasonable goals."

Emotions Raw and Cooked

We do not experience emotions in their rawest state; they always come cooked, prepared with culinary attention by our surrounding culture. We are taught early on how a Christian is to act regarding anger and guilt. And there comes a time when we are invited to learn a more daring embrace of these emotions. We had been taught to pursue a lifestyle of "meek and humble of heart," but there are occasions that call for a fiercer defense of our best values.

A discipline helpful here is the strategy of naming and taming our powerful emotions. This is an exercise in befriending an unsettling emotion. A painful feeling stirs in the dark corner of your heart. Hidden in the shadows, protected from the light of speech, a "negative" emotion exerts its frightening force. We feel miserable; but is this misery fear or guilt or resentment? Naming an emotion includes reaching the deep theme. When I am chronically irritated in traffic, what is taking place? The irritation (anger) may come from impatience; as my wife has observed, I expect all the traffic lights to turn green when I approach. Admitting this is embarrassing but eases the demand to have things go my way.

Naming an emotion goes a long way to taming it. Recognizing the energy that propels this emotion also releases its power over one. Words wrestle our feelings out of darkness, helping us befriend our emotional life. This befriending does not take away the distress but gives it a name. It is no longer necessary to hold it off, or hold it down, or hold it still.

Passion and Self-Control

The story of passion in the early centuries of Christianity revolved around the stoic question of self-control, the very masculine ideal of a serene command of one's world. Augustine fell victim to this ideal, so unlike the passionate life of Jesus. Augustine was explicit about this ideal of self-control. "What friend of wisdom and holy joys who being married . . . would not prefer, if this were possible, to beget children without this lust, so that in this function of begetting offspring, the members created for this purpose should not be stimulated by the heat of lust, but should be actuated by his volition" (*The City of God*).

Critics have pointed out the root of Augustine's anxiety. Anglican theologian Sarah Coakley: "Even normal marital sexual activity is intrinsically worrisome to Augustine because of the revolt of the male body—the phallus—against the man's rational will to have complete control over himself." Religion scholar Christina Traina adds, "A will preoccupied with its own actions is in the end narrow and egocentric." Such a person will tend to see others as a threat to this ideal of self-control.

Anger—An Emergency Passion

Anger often arises as an emergency emotion: provoked by sudden threat, resolved by swift response. After we respond to some threat, our body again begins to relax. (Would that it were that easy!) But it may be that our anger is still aroused, smoldering as it were in rehearsals of passive-aggressive responses. Willard Gaylin: "Fear and anger are designed to serve as responses to threats to our survival. To our survival—not to our pride, status, position, manhood or dignity."

Christian piety has often seen anger as a sin, an emotion to be avoided at all costs. Yet in the Bible we meet Yahweh's wrath and Jesus's anger. We learn there is a just anger but struggle to distinguish it from "righteous indignation" when our pride is affronted.

In our workshops participants were asked to "major" in one specific emotion. Each year a number of men in the group would choose anger since it was a regular source of trouble in their lives. But after reading about shame they chose to change their major. They had come to identify their core emotion as shame, often arising from a home life of alcoholism or poverty or anxiety about sexuality. When they felt ashamed they often reacted with strategies of angry behavior. (Anger is a hedge against humiliation.) They reported that once they had named this core emotion accurately, their anger had greatly decreased. Coming to terms with their shame, such angry defenses were less necessary.

Others who had "majored" in loneliness began to recognize the harsh judgments they regularly made of themselves whenever they were alone. "Unattractive, abandoned, etc." Now they were coming to see that this aloneness could be embraced as something closer to solitude.

The Chinese language catches the ambiguity of these passions. Patience or perseverance is expressed in Chinese as a knife blade hovering over the heart. But is this the blade of an attacker or of a surgeon? Does it draw near to injure or to heal? We learn the purpose of the blade only when we hold still (there is that metaphor of "holding" again) long enough to recognize its intent.

Our colleague James Zullo added to our discussion the suggestion that painful emotions have their distinctive "AIM." They begin in arousal (A), disrupting our peace while trying to get our attention. They then require interpretation (I): what is this arousal telling me? Third, they move us (M) to action, to do something about our distress.

Benefits of the Painful Emotions

Anger challenges me to right a wrong; calls for decisive action to protect from harm something that I judge to be of genuine value.

Anger can lead to action in pursuit of justice

Shame affirms the necessary boundaries that support our sense of self; warns of the risks of premature exposure; protects the privacy that makes genuine intimacy possible.

Shame is one of the roots of personal dignity

Guilt reminds us of the shape of our best self; alerts us to discrepancies between ideals and behavior; defends the commitments and value choices through which we give meaning to life.

Guilt often supports our sense of personal integrity.

Loneliness passes judgment on our interpersonal world, signaling that our links with others are not sustaining us; feeling alone can move us to take action to strengthen our relationships. It is a response to being alone.

Loneliness can be an ally in our search for intimacy

Fear warns us of possible danger; alerts us "ahead of time"; this serves as a way we carry the wisdom of our past experience into the future.

Fear is a component of mature courage.

Grief ignites the dreadful feeling that something essential is perishing; prompts us to evaluate what must be held onto and what must be let go; moves us toward a future both uncharted and full of promise.

Through lamentation grief opens us to genuine hope.

Guardians of Our Belonging

A second choice for a focus in the workshop turned out to be shame. We had initially not included it since it did not seem an important part of our own life. A participant approached us mid-workshop asking: "when will we look at shame?" For him shame was central, and his concern convinced us to include it in our reflections.

A first challenge was to recognize how both shame and guilt are guardians of our belonging. The emotion of guilt arises when we fail our own best values. When we recognize the boundary of our commitments we become able to distinguish healthy guilt—regret for a specific action and asking forgiveness—from an unhealthy sense of guiltiness—feeling guilty for the bad weather that spoils the picnic, as though I had some control over the climate. Christians have often learned to feel guilty for the stirrings that make us human.

We found that most participants in our courses had come to terms with the emotion of guilt; a more pernicious passion was shame. This emotion is about exposure—being seen when we are not ready. Being out of step, embarrassed for a moment after I have made some inappropriate remark. Shame patrols the boundary of our belonging in our social world. In the past some men have adopted the strategy of composure: showing a well-guarded presence among others, intent on not being exposed and embarrassed.

The puzzlement of shame lies in its many meanings. It might name a humiliating exposure, but it also names a positive attention to boundaries. "Have you no sense of shame?" Shaming is also part of that social belittling when we mock or insult others. Here not just an emotion but a sin.

From Loneliness to Solitude

Novelist Anne Proulx got it about right in describing the hero of her story *The Shipping News*: "Quoyle was a failure at loneliness, yearned to be gregarious, to know his company was a pleasure to others."

Loneliness is a bad feeling about something good—our relationship with others. This emotion questions our connection with others. Perhaps our ties are too few; perhaps they are superficial. Maybe we are asking too much from people, or are settling for too little.

There are times when loneliness seems appropriate. The teenager edging away from childhood and a dependence on her parents that once was natural. Or a person is moving to a new city for a new job, leaving behind a rich network of reliable friends. Or after the death of a spouse or close friend, the feeling of an emotional void.

This emotion becomes destructive when it makes harsh judgments. I am alone because I am unattractive, don't know how to make friends. Now this emotion is punishment. But loneliness can be an ally of intimacy, inviting us to examine our relationship, risking new ones, letting go those with too much dependence built in.

Loneliness may include an invitation to solitude—a deeper comfort with being alone. In the midst of an important transition in work or love, we find we can survive by ourselves. We do not need to fill every moment with social media or other noise. We can tolerate the stillness that arises at different times in life.

The Christian script for solitude reminds us that Jesus's public life began and ended in this mood. At the beginning he was led by the Spirit into the desert, finding himself alone where he had to face important questions. At his approaching death a more traumatic aloneness: "why have you abandoned me?" In between these two experiences Jesus at times needed to be alone. "He withdrew from there in a boat to a deserted place by himself." Like us, he needed periods of quiet and retreat, time to think things over, to savor what could not be digested on the run or in a crowd. Like Jesus, we need to learn how to live with others and at times, to do without them.

Psychologist Adam Phillips muses on solitude as a potentially fatal journey since we do not thrive apart from a supportive community. Yet there are moments when we need to risk "withdrawals from human company (in search of) a replenishing privacy." We had read in Scripture that it is not good to be alone, but life has taught us that at times it is necessary and even healing.

CHAPTER SIX

The Marriage of Eros and Grace

It is only in and through the body that we experience grace. (religion scholar Christina Traina)

Through the decades of the '80s and '90s we continued to offer a course on the painful emotions, and separately, another on a spirituality of sexuality. The course on the emotions originated with a focus on anger, shame, and loneliness and later expanded to include guilt, fear, and depression and led to two books: *Shadows of the Heart* (1994) and *Transforming the Painful Emotions* (2010). The course on sexuality led to *A Sense of Sexuality* (1989) and then *Wisdom of the Body* (2001).

Gradually we realized that emotions and sexuality are both rooted in that vital energy that the Western tradition has named *eros*. For decades this term had suffered from negative nuances in Christian circles, conjuring up seedy bookstores and "erotic" novels. The church had contributed to this bias by suggesting there was an antagonism between a spiritual (non-sexual) affection and a more grasping sexual attraction. In this dualistic vision *agape* named this spiritual relationship and *eros* pointed to a more fleshly stirring.

Pope Benedict XVI, in his first pastoral letter—"God Is Love" (2005)—sought to rescue *eros* from its negative meaning, restoring its original healthy meaning of passionate affection. More than twenty times the pope praises this vital force in creation that is an aspect of God's passionate love for creation. God's love is deeply spiritual (*agape*) but also *eros*—a passionate longing to embrace us.

For many today, eros and grace still seem unlikely marriage partners. They come from different neighborhoods, *eros* associated with the flesh and grace exiled in heaven. How could they make a life together? We may need to see that eros is spiritual energy and grace is embodied. Seen in this light, they have been engaged for a long time.

Eros is the dynamic energy that courses through the world, animating every living thing. It is the force that turns the flower to the sun, the energy that stirs humans to be in touch, to reach out and link their lives in lasting ways. Eros is the raw energy that impels the infant to seize a bright marble lying in the dirt and put it in her mouth. Eros wants to touch, to taste, and even to consume.

Eros is our desire for closeness, the visceral hope that moves us out of solitude and motivates us to chance the risky relationships of friendship and love. Eros is about union—with the beautiful other, with a suffering person, with the world of nature waiting to be embraced and protected.

Eros is the force that quickens our hearts when we encounter suffering and moves us to help and heal. Sex, curiosity, compassion—eros moves through our lives in delightful and bewildering ways. To live a responsible life we will have to name and even tame this ambiguous force.

Then there is grace, at play in our embodied selves,
making our lives graceful, gracious, and grateful.

Behold a graceful dancer. Her body moves in a fluid rhythm. We know that her leaps and turns must be long rehearsed, but they seem free and spontaneous. This sensual movement stirs our hearts with delight as the dancer's body moves like a prayer.

Behold a gracious host. As you enter his home you initially feel ill at ease among so many guests. The host welcomes you and takes your coat. He points out friends in the room and eases your discomfort.

Behold how we gratify in the flesh. Washing a fevered body and changing soiled bed linens for sheets that are fresh and clean, we gratify a suffering person. Rubbing lotion on a stiff back evokes groans of gratitude; this is sensual grace. *Charis* is the Greek term for embodied grace in which flesh and spirit embrace. Gratitude is the evoked emotion that binds pleasure to gratefulness.

The Body Symbolic

Our body is more than mute matter, more even than flesh and blood. It speaks for us in groans and sighs—often too deep for words, as St. Paul wrote. Breaking into a sweat tells the world something about us, even if we would prefer the world not know. Most especially our bodily gestures—a slight bow to someone we respect, a comforting hand on the shoulder of a distressed friend—speak volumes, though the sound is off. Our bodies are symbolic in three distinct ways, announcing to the world something about our hidden heart: ornamental, instrumental, sacramental.

The Body Ornamental

We love to adorn our bodies, whether with war paint or eyeliner. From jewelry to tattoos we demonstrate our impulse toward adornment. We delight in accessorizing our body. Let's face it: we like to show off.

The cardinals in my backyard and the Cardinals in the Vatican share this impulse to display their brilliant plumage. Even in biblical texts we meet this inclination: "Your cheeks are beautiful with ornaments, your neck with strings of jewels. We will make you ornaments of gold, studded with silver" (Song of Songs 1:10-11).

This inclination can turn obsessive, as fashion dictates ever more glam, but the universal desire to have our body speak for us endures.

The Body Instrumental

In our youth we may be especially attuned to our body ornamental. It is, after all, the time for dating, which may require extra makeup. And in our thirties and forties we become more aware of our body as an instrument: a source of stamina, more attentive to diet, needful of warm clothes in winter—even if bulky jackets are unfashionable.

Now we may be more concerned with keeping in shape, with our body as the means of "getting things done." We become more aware how vulnerable we are as embodied creatures. We pay more attention to our body's needs. Our bodies are, of course, more than mere instruments, but instruments they are.

The Body Sacramental

Our bodies are instruments and also ornaments, and they are sacraments that announce and celebrate God's grace. The most dramatic instance of this sacred character is in love making: our fragile, awkward bodies come together to share affection that goes beyond words. This is certainly where eros and grace embrace.

A sacrament is a near occasion of grace, a ritual gesture or physical action through which we enter more deeply into the presence of God. When young we learned that sacraments effect what they signify: they nourish and reconcile. It was probably in religious rituals that we first learned that our body was meant to be ornamental: the priest garbed in vibrant colors at Easter. Even the lowly altar boy might feel some of this. "Mass was the ballet of my youth . . . [this was] a world where your body was less visible but where your movement was more noticeable." An aging altar boy looks back, "Within these sacred robes, an altar boy's body became a stage prop. Even a young, shapeless youth could feel in his flesh that his movement was grand and dramatic. The bows, the genuflections, the well-timed turns—all these were part of a great sacred drama" (John Schekleton, "Homosexuality and the Priesthood," *Commonweal* [November 22, 1996], pp. 15–18).

Religious scholar Christina Traina traces the connection between the body and our sacramental heritage: "It is only in and through the body that we experience grace; therefore the body has sacramental significance." She reminds us: "We wash and we are baptized; we eat and we partake of Eucharist; we touch to heal . . . our tradition also teaches that in marriage the union of bodies is a sign and symbol of grace that is really present."

Bringing Grace Down to Earth: Presence and Absence

Ours is a God of presence—often a sudden, surprising presence that appears in the midst of absence. It was in the desert that our ancestors became aware of a presence—*Shekinah*—that would lead them to a land of milk and honey. Before God had a face or a gender, God was mysterious presence. When clouds moved they sensed it was time to break camp (Exodus 40:36).

After Jesus's death his absence was broken by sudden appearances: once at dawn to ask his friends, "What's for breakfast?" (John 21:4), once in the evening at dinner time (Luke 24:30). His presence was startling and nourishing all at once.

At Pentecost the disciples had gathered in an upper room from which Jesus was conspicuously absent, a domestic desert. His absence—a generous absence—opened space for the Spirit to appear, enheartening the befuddled disciples.

A Prayer of Presence

God of Israel, God of Jesus, your name is Shekinah, presence. We feel your saving presence in our bodies, our emotions, our hopes.

You appear in deserts and oases, in crises and at quiet meals. Your epiphanies calm our fears and heal our shame.

Help us to recognize you in all your faces—in the flesh as well as in the spirit, in eros as well as in logos.

Help us remember that Jesus is God's desire in the flesh, God's body language. Make us alive to our world, and through it, alert to your presence.

A Prayer of Absence

God of presence, help us to bear your mysterious absence.

Help us through the darkness of the nights when we cannot see you, the discontents of winters when we cannot feel you, the sorrow of seasons when we cannot hear you.
Attune us to the absence that is generous—emptying us of a cherished past in preparation for your surprising future.

Lead us not into despair, but toward the hope of your coming.

Bringing Grace Down to Earth: Feasting and Fasting

We feast both to celebrate and give thanks. Public festivities grace the yearly calendar in every nation. In harvest festivals, we recognize survival and bounty. When we feast, we do more than simply take in nourishment; we make a celebration in our eating. We bring out candles, a special tablecloth, the good wine. If the food satisfies our nutritional needs, feasting nourishes other famished aspects of our lives—especially our hunger for community and delight. Festivals and carnivals testify that the human spirit needs regularly to indulge. Without the occasional feast, our souls begin to starve.

At its best, feasting is a disciplined performance. A banquet proceeds as a leisurely pace, making "fast food" seem out of place. Since a major portion of our delight comes in sharing the occasion with those we love, we rarely feast alone. A feast is not an orgy; we do not abandon ourselves to food or drink or sex. Genuine feasting, in fact, teaches us to avoid excess. When it degenerates into a display of mindless abandon or conspicuous consumption, a party somehow fails as a feast.

The Christian liturgy offers the example of a holy feast. We prepare colorful vestments and banners, add incense and song, and celebrate in unison our blessings and our grief. Along with other feasts, liturgical celebrations—when not reduced to repetitive or empty gestures—instruct us in an important truth: feasting is a communal art, not a private indulgence.

Without feasts, the soul begins to starve.

We feast not just with food and drink, but with all our senses. Listening to a symphony or attending an opera provides a feast for the soul; a hot bath is a more humble but no less sensual feast for the body. At a museum, we feast our eyes on art that others have created. But plagued by the busyness of our lives, we may fail to feast. Weighed down with work and worry, we insist we have no time for such luxuries. But eventually, deprived of this nourishment, our souls begin to shrink.

Feasting is meant to be a part of our sexual lives as well. Feasting in our sexuality both expresses a basic instinct and celebrates something more. Lovemaking brings the shared play of pleasure, and we give thanks. Savoring our mutual delight, we recognize that sex serves more than reproduction or private relief. As with food and drink, we learn that the feast is ruined when sex is used manipulatively or its pleasure is abused. In our sexuality, too, the feast refuses both denial and excess.

Long married couples come, somewhat ruefully, to recognize a new discipline in their sexual feast. As children and pets populate the household, as everyday errands and second jobs fill the weekly schedules, busy parents check calendars to find time to spend together. Now the spontaneity of earlier romance gives way to the necessity of "scheduled" lovemaking . . . a new rhythm in the sexual dance of mid-life intimacy.

In the life of eros, feasting is not abandonment to the flesh. As a Christian discipline, feasting is a response to the gift of creation. If we carry wounds in our sexual lives, feasting can be a healing exercise. With courage and support, we slowly relearn the goodness of our sensuality. We devote time now to re-creation—through music or exercise or quiet time alone. We prepare a special meal to share with friends; we welcome the reverent touch of massage. As we learn to feast in our erotic lives, pleasure returns to a rightful place of honor.

Welcome to the Fast

With its many delights and necessary disciplines, feasting is part of the rhythm of eros. This movement of eros finds its complement in fasting. Fasting has been seen as an exotic exercise, suited to monks, nuns, and other religious elites, but not for ordinary folks like us. Today, we recognize fasting as an ordinary discipline, part of every life.

> *In fasting we interrupt an ordinary rhythm in our life,*
> *so that we may listen to other longings.*

In the contemporary retrieval of fasting as a healthy discipline, we find a richer motivation. Fasting is not meant as a repudiation of the body and its passions, nor should it spring from a desire to punish a guilty soul. Fasting is an exercise of concentration, not deprivation.

Unavoidably a rush of duty and delight fills our lives; each day overflows with demands of what has to be done. These demands are often good in themselves, but their insistence crowds out other hopes and dreams. To fast is to rest briefly, in the midst of busy lives, in order to attune our hearts to neglected possibilities. Fasting practices us in paying attention, so that we may be more present to our heart's desires.

Fasting is long cherished in the traditions of the East. As Western Christians return to the experience, we recognize how strangely nourishing a period of fasting can be. Interrupting the ordinary rhythms of our lives makes us more alert, more awake. This may be rooted in the physiology of fasting: jolted by a lack of food, the body goes on alert. But getting past the initial alarm, we come to appreciate the emptiness—in spirit as much as in body. Those who fast report their senses are sharpened and their minds less distracted, as the overwhelming burdens of daily routine seem to melt away.

In fasting, we say "no" to some part of our experience in order to protect the deeper "yes" of our lives. This can happen in quite ordinary ways. In order to be fully attentive at an important evening meeting, we skip our usual glass of wine with dinner. Finding that a weekend spent watching televised sports dulls our sense and distracts us from family activities, we cut back on TV time in favor of richer pleasures.

The fast is an ordinary part of our sexual life as well. Our partner is away on a business trip or we are struggling with illness. So we fast from our regular pattern of love-making. Those who embrace a life of committed celibacy recognize that their fast from sexual sharing benefits from a life enriched by genuine friendship and the sensual delights of music, art, and beauty. Fasting from sexual contact in a belief that eros is evil is not a Christian discipline but an unhealthy flight from creation.

With Aloysius Jin, S.J., Catholic bishop of Shanghai

Part Three

Eros with Wrinkles

CHAPTER SEVEN

"Waiting for Someone to Take Him to China"—The 1990s

Is it not a pleasure to study with dedication and practice? Is it not a delight when friends come from afar to visit? (Confucius, *The Analects* 1.1)

At dawn of the sixth day of the lunar New Year 1994, our ferry slipped out of Victoria Harbor in Hong Kong and headed for the mouth of the Pearl River. Passing Macau, the boat carrying three hundred Chinese and us four Westerners turned north into the river, passing near Shang Chuan Island, where the Jesuit Francis Xavier had died in 1552 at the age of forty-two, as it says in the guidebook, "waiting for someone to take him to China." Now, to our great surprise, we had found someone to take us to China.

Three hours later we arrived at our first destination, the town where the Jesuit Matteo Ricci, born the year Xavier had died, would spend the early years of his life in China. So began our unlikely pilgrimage into mainland China.

Our trip had been occasioned by Sister Mary Olga Lam, who was principal of a middle school in Hong Kong. She had attended our course on the emotions at Loyola in Chicago the previous year and had invited us to provide a similar course for Catholic educators in her own city. Following the workshop she had invited us and several others to accompany her on a short excursion into the mainland, where she had grown up. During the few days of this trip unanticipated feelings stirred within us, and we experienced what felt like a summons to return and spend much of our sixties in this land.

The account of our subsequent twelve years of teaching in mainland China is a story of serendipity, unlikely adventures, and surprising encounters. It was, most of all, one of those "coincidences in our favor" that shaped a decade of our life.

Coincidences Begin

Returning from our first short trip into the mainland we stopped in San Francisco to attend the funeral of a good friend. Since we were in that city we decided to visit Father Ed Malatesta, yet another Jesuit who had begun a kind of boutique center at the University of San Francisco—the Ricci Institute for the study of China and Christianity. He introduced us to a Protestant group (the United Board for Christian Higher Education in China) that sponsored Christian educators who would spend their sabbatical year teaching in China. This group took us on as their token Catholics and sponsored our yearly trips to China, opening doors at universities for us over the next decade.

Apart from our public role as scholars we were practicing Catholics and were blessed to be introduced to a number of vital Catholic families and through them the Catholic bishop of Shanghai, Aloysius Jin, S.J. The bishop's career unfolded through the upheavals of twentieth-century Chinese history: ordained a priest in the late 1940s, he was sent to Europe to gain a PhD in theology. While there he learned French, German, and Italian and met some of the European Jesuits who were introducing the ideas that would underpin Vatican II, still a decade away. Returning home, he fell victim to the Communist purge of Catholic leadership in Shanghai in 1953. Only after more than twenty years of prison and house arrest was he able to initiate his leadership in the city of Shanghai. A major task would be regaining the property of Catholic parishes seized by the Communist state. Over the next decades he managed to regain control of the cathedral (previously a warehouse) and boost the number of active parishes from a dozen to more than a hundred.

The Women of Shanghai

In the early 1990s the bishop began sending lay women to Notre Dame in preparation for their taking up leadership roles in the diocese of Shanghai. Cecilia Tao Beiling arrived at the University of Notre Dame to study in 1994. We became close friends as we learned of her family's history while accompanying her as she studied theology here. Returning home to Shanghai she took up the work of deputy editor at Guang Qi Press, the largest Catholic publishing house in China. Cecilia oversaw projects like the translation of Richard McBrien's *Catholicism.*

At a lunch meeting with faculty at Fudan, where we were teaching in 1998, we met a young scholar by the name of Rachel Zhu Xiaohong. Rachel had just finished her dissertation—at this Communist university—on the Catholic theologian Edward Schillebeeckx. She spoke English very well and was—the surprises kept coming— a Catholic. Over the next decade we would often spend dinners with her, her husband, Daniel, and their two sons, Ivan and James.

A third surprising companion that came into our life in these years was the artist Teresa Wo Ye. After studying at St. John's University in Collegeville, Minnesota, Teresa returned to Shanghai and began an ambitious project of designing and replacing the stained-glass windows in the cathedral that had been destroyed in the Cultural Revolution (1966–1976). Evelyn was instrumental in convincing the Jesuit artist Tom Lucas to assist her in this task.

Yet another coincidence intervened when we met professor Fan Lizhu, a sociologist of religion, who had just begun teaching at Fudan herself. Soon Fan, Evelyn, and I were meeting weekly to discuss places where Chinese popular religion—her specialty—seemed to resonate with aspects of Christian faith.

During the first decade of the new century we taught a number of courses in the sociology of religion at Fudan University in Shanghai. The city itself was a lesson in urban life as more and more people migrated from the countryside to take jobs in the new factories that continued to be built. One day we were standing at a busy intersection with professor Fan and, attempting hyperbole, I remarked on the multitude of bicycles waiting for the traffic light to change. "A city of ten million bikes!" I dramatically exclaimed. Fan responded, "No. There are certainly more than that."

Our experiences with students—eager, bright, friendly—were a constant source of delight. They were the offspring of parents who had survived the Cultural Revolution by avoiding any expression of religion; they themselves were innocent of any explicit religiousness. When

Evelyn helped a student improve her writing style while looking over the short essay she had written, she urged the student to bring to the essay more than quotes and summaries of scholars; perhaps some of her own ideas or insights? The student, surprised, responded, "What if I am wrong?"

As the twentieth-century began, China realized that its educational structure was decidedly medieval. A yearly national exam on China's history was still in place, taking up the space where universities might have flourished. Beijing University, the premier educational center of the nation, had been founded only a year before the twentieth century began. At that time in Shanghai the French Jesuits (once again the Jesuits) established Aurora University—French for "dawn" or "sunrise." Unfortunately the school was Francophile in the extreme—all but ignoring the Chinese culture and language. This led a young Chinese Jesuit, Ma Shangbo, to leave the Jesuits and helped found an alternate university a few years later, naming it Fudan—"second dawn." Today this university is regularly ranked among the top three centers of education, along with Beijing University and science-centered Tsinghua University in Beijing.

A Buddhist Restaurant

In October 2003, Professor Fan took us to visit Shenzhen, now a city of seven million that had been for centuries a sleepy fishing village near Hong Kong. When Deng Xiaoping in 1979 opened China to a new economic model closer to capitalism, entrepreneurs of every stripe raced to this city to buy up farmland where factories appeared almost overnight (think Apple, Microsoft, Amazon, etc.). Fan had researched, as part of her PhD work at the University of Hong Kong, how citizens of Shenzhen, in a milieu of raw vitality and what journalist Ian Buruma named "the wild, wild East," made sense of their new cultural world and how aspects of popular religion helped in such transitions.

The first day we visited a new, attractive Catholic Church. When we expressed our amazement at such a building in a Communist country Fan explained that it was part of the "show" for visitors from Hong Kong and the West. "See how tolerant we are." The second day we visited a Buddhist temple that was teeming with visitors lighting josh sticks of incense and praying before various shrines. Fan explained that most of the visitors were not, in fact, Buddhists but ordinary Chinese choosing this religious site for their own spiritual purposes—whether praying that their pregnant daughter might have a son or that their new business might succeed.

The third day we went to a Buddhist restaurant that was quite different from Western bistros. Spiritual reading material filled a number of shelves in the large entryway. The waitress warned us, somewhat sternly, to order only what we would eat. This alert pointed to a "no takeaways" and a Buddhist concern to avoid waste. The restaurant was vegetarian, of course. The place was so engaging that it became the centerpiece of two essays that the three of us later wrote about this fascinating city.

On our last day in Shenzhen we were introduced to a Buddhism-based ritual that has become popular in contemporary China—the freeing of living things (*fang sheng*). A small group might gather at a lake side with a Buddhist monk. After several prayers or spiritual readings, each person there would release some small animal, a pet turtle or fish, or perhaps a dove. This ritual celebrated the right of all living things to be free. And the event reminded members of the group to be more mindful of fellow creatures and less possessive.

Later that October we traveled by train two hours south of Shanghai to Zhejiang University, where we met a number of "culture Christians"—scholars who were committed to Christian values but for the sake of preserving their jobs did not join any Christian community or publicly confess Christian beliefs. An excellent example of such a culture Christian was a young scholar in the philosophy department who was teaching a course on "Classics of Western Philosophy." When we inquired which classics these were, we learned that his classes included lectures on St. John's Gospel and St. Augustine. Western classics, indeed.

Our more academic challenge at Fudan University was to explore with Professor Fan aspects of China's popular religion. One of these was an attentiveness to seemingly chance events that become influential in a person's life. This awareness—*yuan fen* in Chinese—might arise in meeting another person by coincidence and eventually marrying this person, or it might involve losing a job when such a loss opened the door to a better and more fulfilling career. Were these merely random events or were they more than chance, or at least "coincidences in our favor"? For both Chinese and Christians, such turns of events might invite a greater sense of responsibility in responding to these gifts.

Another aspect of Chinese popular religiousness was a sense of destiny—*ming yun* in Chinese. If one part of life was shaped by time and place, family, and gender (fate or *ming*), another part arose from personal initiative (*yun*). Chinese name the more "fated" part of life as *tianming*—heaven's will. The personal choices of vocation or career they speak of as *yun*—the individual circumstances and choices that shape one's destiny. For centuries the Chinese like other ethnic groups accepted their fortune—born in this land on this farm at this time—as what had to be—their fate. Amid the enormous changes taking place in contemporary China many young people, growing up on a small farm, were seeing new possibilities in risking a move to the city in hopes of finding a job that could change their destiny. They talk today of "grasping their fate" (*baowo mingyun*).

Perhaps the most striking coincidence in our favor was the timing of the introduction of courses on religion in Chinese universities. These institutions had long ignored "religion," seeing it through the Marxist lens of "an opiate for the people." By the late 1990s, professors returning from foreign trips reported that every major university in the world had the academic study of religion (whether called religious studies, or theology departments, or divinity schools). Perhaps it was time for Chinese universities, however steeped in Marxism, to begin to offer these courses. Professors were becoming more attuned to the deep cultural values that the study of religion often highlight. In our last years in China a new concentration—*xue guo*, or "Study of the National Heritage"—opened an avenue for the academic study of the Confucian and Daoist heritages, now recognized as both cultural and religious.

Coincidences in Hong Kong

Yet another coincidence in our favor during these years took place when we met up again in Hong Kong with Victoria Yeung, who had studied with us in Chicago. Victoria is a dynamic lay leader in the diocese who helps direct a lay education program at Holy Spirit Study Centre. Each Easter week for the first decade of the new century we offered a week-long course for several hundred highly motivated Catholic teachers and nurses and lawyers in the city.

Soon we were repeating these lectures at a Protestant center for spirituality, *Dao Feng Shan*. (The title translates as mountain (*shan*) of the Way and Spirit (*dao feng*). Here too we had the opportunity to talk with pastors and religious educators who were developing a Christian spirituality that better fit their ethnic heritage.

After my brief study of Chinese culture and religion in the 1970s I had turned to pursue what seemed like a very different vocation in pastoral theology. I had said goodbye to China. Now in the 2000s we found ourselves teaching in China.

CHAPTER EIGHT

Retirement: "We Have Begun Our Initial Descent"

It had been a long but satisfying trip. As the plane from Seoul Korea approached Chicago the pilot announced, "We have begun our initial descent. Those who will be leaving us here, welcome home."

Seoul Korea was magnificent. Every bit the equal of Hong Kong. What a change from my time there fifty years ago. Now in the last days of May in the year of the Lord 2010 we were almost finished with the week-long lectures on a spirituality of the emotions when a virus found its home in my left vocal chord.

At first only a sore throat; then I lost my voice. Then the virus went to work throughout my body. Evelyn completed the lectures, as I was busy being sick. A clinic at the airport was a godsend, and with some medication I managed the ten-hour flight back to Chicago. We had scheduled a two-week rest period before our summer course at Loyola would begin. I thought this would be sufficient for a full recovery. I was wrong.

Evelyn carried the load in our two-week Loyola course as the virus held on through the summer and thoughts of retirement began to stir. We were both now seventy years old, and the bit of Chinese wisdom I revered more than followed returned: "Know when enough is enough."

As we pondered what retirement might look like, a "last project" appeared on the horizon, surfacing in a course we were doing on a spirituality of sexuality. As usual we included a session on Christians and homosexuality. Once upon a time—in the 1980s—this had been a challenging presentation. Now the younger members in the course thanked us and seemed to say, "Been there; done that."

It was time to move on. Catholics today were eager to better understand what it means to be transgender. It seemed natural for us to turn to this question; events in American culture were making space for such a conversation.

In 1982 Julie Andrews, with impeccable credentials as a woman in *The Sound of Music*, could cut her hair short, put on a suit, and pass for Victor as well as Victoria in the movie of that name. This switch of genders was all in good fun. That same year Dustin Hoffman had more work to do to pass as a woman in order to land an acting job in *Tootsie*. A padded bra and more padding around the hips failed to convince in this comedy. By 1999 the mood had become serious, even deadly, when Hilary Swank won an Oscar portraying a young girl hoping to live as a boy in *Boys Don't Cry*.

Meanwhile real people were describing their own transitioning in gender. Jan Morris tells the story in her memoir *Conundrum*, of how in her mid-forties she transitioned from Jim to Jan, while remaining married to her wife, Elizabeth. In a recent interview she writes of their seventy years together and the tombstone they had already prepared in advance, "Here are two friends, at the end of one life." Jennifer Finney Boylan, after gaining tenure at Colby College, transitioned in gender while continuing in her marriage and teaching career. Her frequent op-eds in the *New York Times* give readers a normalizing portrait of how and why such a change might occur.

Neuroscientists were continuing to better understand how hormones shape the earliest stage of the human embryo in the direction of male (testosterone) or female (estrogen). The brain itself, influenced by these hormones, is gendered. A person who is transgendered may well experience a tension between bodily shape and psychic core. The word dysphoria has often been used to describe this tension.

In the Catholic Church, a kind of dueling Bible controversy has arisen. Some believers cling to the literal account in the Book of Genesis of the creation of male and female, with no exceptions. For others this "sacred binary" could be re-imagined as similar to night and day: God created light and dark and everything in between: dawn and dusk, twilight and sundown. Our lives are many splendored, not black and white.

Other Catholics draw attention to St. Paul's judgment: "There is no longer Jew or Greek, no longer slave or free; no longer male or female, for you are all one in Jesus Christ" (Galatians 3:28). Does this not suggest that faith delivers us from cultural distinctions and their force?

Christians look to the Bible for ethical norms, while the sacred text turns repeatedly not to the ordinary or the normal (stay in your lane), but to the exceptional, the surprising, the miraculous. We long for the normal, the straight and narrow, but Scripture again and again turns our attention to paradox, reversals of fortune and transformations. Water becomes wine; a blind person sees; Lazarus is raised from the dead. Often it is only later that we admit, "Surely God was in this place and I, I did not know it" (Genesis 28:16).

As we prepared to retire—less travel, fewer workshops—we plunged into the literature around transgender lives. And we met and interviewed transgender persons in our community. A great gift for us was meeting Sister Luisa, who had spent several decades caring for transgender individuals. The story was often the same: a young person fails to fit in with others' expectations of them. They feel compelled to adopt "a false self," trying to please others, even at the expense of their own mental well-being. But in this way lies madness, and, if fortunate, the transgender person begins to affirm his or her genuine self.

This self-acceptance leads to a spiritual transition. One trans person writes, "Transitioning allows us to share with society the gender personality that we have been from the start. It avoids the false selves we have developed to live as others expected us to, based on our external bodies." Another speaks of the inner effect of such a change. "When I finally came out, something incredible was happening in me. For the first time in years, I began to feel that I was becoming part of the human community in an authentic way. Through my vulnerability, fear, and suffering, I was finding God in a way I had never known."

Christian groups vary in their acceptance or rejection of their transgender members. A publication of the Methodist Church, *Made in God's Image*, records, "We understand our gender diversity to be a gift from God, intended to add to the rich variety of human experience and perspective . . . the problem is not in being different, but in living in a fearful, condemning world."

In the summer of 2015 we had the opportunity to present some of these ideas to fellow members of Holy Cross Village. We were accompanied by our new colleague, the transgender activist Meghan Buell. Sixty people attended the discussion; Meghan was the hit as she spoke of her own gender transition, her family's response to her coming out, and her own hopes in establishing the not for profit TREES—Transgender Resources in Education and Enhancement Services. As we go to press with this volume we are celebrating the opening of a downtown office dedicated to these supportive services—fittingly christened *Tree House*.

Retirement

But we were talking of retirement. The thought conjured up (surprise!) scenarios of sunny California. We had worked there at the University of San Francisco through many of the winters of the 2000s and the climate was inviting. But the price: not so much. In our search we ventured a bit north to Santa Rosa, having heard of a retirement community there, only to learn it had been constructed on the San Andreas Fault. Not our fault.

Then we began to see the point of staying close to home. South Bend—its winters notwithstanding—was where our friends lived, where our faith community flourished. So we moved to Holy Cross Village, across the street from the University of Notre Dame, where our teaching had begun.

Enchantment

As we settled into retirement in 2015 our interests diverged for the first time. As Evelyn began exploring the virtues of aging I set out to re-read some of my favorite novels. I began by revisiting Evelyn Waugh's *Brideshead Revisited*. The reading progressed smoothly until page 31 when I came across Waugh's description of the mystery of falling in love. "But I was in search of love in those days, and I went full of curiosity and the faint, unrecognized apprehension that here, at last, I should find that low door in the wall, which others, I knew, had found before me, which opened on an enclosed and enchanted garden."

Why the "low door?" Would entry require some bending? How was the garden both enclosed and enchanted? And why a garden? Did other readers think of another garden, one at the beginning of the human story? I was hooked.

I began to find enchantment everywhere—in art and nature, even in religion. To poet Gerard Manley Hopkins, the whole world was enchanted. "The world is charged with the grandeur of God," but what is this "charge" so obvious to many but invisible to those encased in a disenchanted reality where "what you see is what you get"?

When we are enchanted we are captivated by some part of life that escapes our control. We search for synonyms: entrancing, compelling, even haunting. A novel might examine magical worlds but also "the magic of a subtler kind—hours that seem to mysteriously vanish in shared conversation, loneliness transformed by the alchemy of new friendship."

Wonder seems to be an integral part of enchantment. "We wonder at what we cannot in any sense incorporate, consume, or encompass in our mental categories; we wonder at mystery, at paradox." Catholic philosopher Charles Taylor defines this experience further. "The wonder is not only at the stupendous whole, but at the way in which we emerge, in one way fragile and insignificant, and yet capable of grasping the whole." For Taylor this is its own kind of spirituality. "Belonging to the earth, the sense of our dark genesis, can also be part of Christian faith . . . it is perhaps precisely the ordinary operation of things which constitutes the 'miracle.'"

Two recent novels have gloried in enchantment. In 1978 Mary Gordon published her novel *Final Payments,* which was set in a 1962 church just as the Council had gotten underway. This allowed Gordon to mark off the difference between the faith of young Isabel and her pre-Vatican II father. "He kept intact that interface between the sacred and the secular" and, emphatically, "one did not look for happiness on earth."

Isabel shares none of these traits of her father's Catholicism, but when he suffers a stroke she is stirred by a lethal combination of guilt and devotion and determines to dedicate her life to caring for him. She sees this as a kind of "sanctuary" that is, in fact, a hiding place. "She had bought sanctuary by giving up youth and freedom, sex and life."

After a long absence from the church Isabel returns for the liturgy of Holy Week. The washing of feet at the Thursday ritual, then the physical embrace of the cross on Good Friday triggered in her memories of bathing, shaving, lovingly touching her father's body. The force of these sensual rituals dislodged her from her enforced "sanctuary," setting her free to begin a life with the support and laughter of her friends. Meditating on the woman pouring ointment over Jesus's head, she reminds herself, "We must not deprive ourselves, our loved one, of the luxury of our extravagant affections." And, "I knew now I must open the jar of ointment."

The novels of Marilynne Robinson, at the turn of the century, conjured what she called "rituals of the ordinary." A mother washing her children's clothes and setting them out to dry were such rituals; the force of water and sunlight came to possess holy power.

For both Gordon and Robinson laughter gains a sacramental quality. It illumines our world and lightens the human heart. Saint Augustine had been suspicious of laughter, reading it as laughter at, or shaming ridicule that had tarnished his own youth. In a spirituality attuned to self-abnegation, there was little to laugh about. But these authors lifted up a healthy laughter, a signature of grace itself. "I began to suspect that, as I have from time to time, that grace has a grand laughter in it."

Both novelists described a world lit from within. Water and sunlight and loving touch can suddenly illumine the grace at play in ordinary life. Enchantment here was not generated from on high but was itself the sensual charm breaking forth within our everyday lives.

This only whet my appetite, and I began to work on a second volume. I could now see how enchantment was meant to be part of the Catholic liturgy. "Make holy these gifts" as we pray at the Eucharist implores God to transform ordinary bread and wine until they become for us extraordinary nourishment. This was not the traditional transubstantiation with believers forced to choose between a real presence of Christ in the Eucharist or a mere symbolic presence, but something at once more mysterious and enchanting. The Spirit of God transforms the ordinary into something extraordinary.

This led to yet a third book as I began to see enchantment everywhere in creation. So in the Prologue to *The Grace of Enchantment*, we wrote,

> We utter the words "I do" of a marriage vow. These are only words; the world remains the same. Yet we are changed, choose to be changed. This is what humans can do. Marriage is an enchantment and something terribly real. . . .
>
> On Ash Wednesday we press ashes on our foreheads and utter, "ashes to ashes, dust to dust," not in stoic defeat but with some barely understood defiance: we humble ourselves to dirt while signaling to ourselves and others that we aspire to life beyond ashes. Let ashes, despite the evidence, not be the end.
>
> We approach a large cross in the liturgy of Good Friday and touch it with reverence. It is just a piece of wood, but we make it more than that. We lavish this wood with memories of life and death, of Jesus's suffering, until this wood is made holy for the life of the world. This is a real presence; this is something we can do.

Enchantment is not delivered from on high: it arises from within this broken world. Blessed and broken. It does not depend on a departure from the flesh, but in an electric meeting of the sensual and the spiritual.

CHAPTER NINE

Annunciation: Illness and Death

An annunciation ... breaking into the small house of our cautionary being. If we have heard rightly the wing-beat and provocation of that visit, the house is no longer habitable in quite the same way as it was before. (George Steiner, *Real Presences*, 143)

March 25, 2015.
The Feast of the Annunciation

We are at our yearly visit to our doctor, whom I had warned about Evelyn's increasing memory problems. He questions her for a few minutes. The day of the week? The month? Then he writes in her chart, *Alzheimers.*

There had been earlier annunciations. We were attending a banquet at Loyola University, from which we were retiring after forty-five years. The date was October 30, 2014, five months before the doctor visit. There was an announcement of a scholarship we had arranged in the name of a beloved executive secretary at the Institute of Pastoral Studies. It had been an emotional and gratifying event, with colleagues assuring us that they would add to the scholarship.

The next morning as we stirred from the bed in our hotel room, Evelyn asked, "Did they announce the scholarship last night?" I was startled. Of the events of the prior evening Evelyn had no memory.

And there would be one more annunciation. This was a visit, some months later, when we consulted a neurologist who led Evelyn through an elaborate neurological exam. His subsequent diagnosis: Evelyn was "on the cusp of an incipient dementia, probably of an Alzheimer's style."

The feast of the Annunciation: The day that Christians remember that shocking moment when Mary discovered she was pregnant with Jesus. From that defining moment Christians would watch for other annunciations—of events that would enchant or stagger them.

Symptoms Abounding

As anyone with a loved one who is suffering memory loss is aware, one of the first symptoms is what we might name migrating dishware. For many years the cups and glasses in the kitchen had been kept in this cabinet; the dishes in that cabinet. Now there is doubt. Where did we put the silverware? Where did the frying pan go? And the shampoo that used to be under the sink? If these moments give a jolt at least to the partner, it is usually managed with humor.

More painful forgetting would come after an evening with dear friends among whom we had all shared many meaningful reflections. The next day Evelyn did not recall any of the conversation. Soon, directions while driving became a challenge. The way to the store, taken a thousand times in our forty-five years in South Bend, was no longer clear.

More painful yet was the ending of our shared writing. For decades we had delighted in shaping new ideas into lectures, then these lectures into essays or chapters of a new book. It was our pleasure and our identity. That was now coming to an end. Evelyn had turned to a possible manuscript on the virtues of aging. We would talk about the strengths that seem to enjoy a special season in our senior years: patience, humor, solitude. But our discussions this time did not lead to paragraphs, pages, or an essay. When friends asked what we were writing about, Evelyn would say, "the virtues of aging." It was not so.

The biggest challenge for me during these months was the repeated questioning. Within a ten-minute period she might ask several times what we were doing next. Early on my exasperation would lead to the tight-throated reply, "as I just said . . ." She would be hurt by my reply, and I soon realized that the only change here would have to be mine. I had to remind myself the memory loss was not a lack of attention; her brain was simply no longer holding on to details from five minutes ago. My patience—supposedly a virtue of aging—came under repeated scrutiny. Slowly, very slowly, I was being instructed in the virtue of patience.

Musings on Memory Lane

"It's a new day." The banal observation now took on new meaning. I came to realize that this was now especially true for Evelyn. Not remembering the details of the day before, she faced each day anew. The old adage about living in the present took on new force. For forty-five years we had relished living in the past—recalling earlier customs in the church that had shaped the piety of the time—

and also living in the future—marking our three-year calendars as we planned our next lecture or travel. In our retirement, time was being compressed into the present.

I came to realize Evelyn had few worries. Worries arise when we begin to fret about some past event or future happening. No longer consciously attuned to either past or future, Evelyn lived in the present. She was living a new kind of innocence, untroubled. Nor was Evelyn frustrated, as I first thought she must be. I would notice her studying her monthly calendar in her office. She seemed to puzzle over it. I began to realize she was trying to recall what those annotations meant. But she was not frustrated. She had forgotten forgetting; it was not the loss for her that it was for me.

Fifty Years of Mutuality

When memory abandons one of us, much is lost. Perhaps for us the greatest loss was the mutuality of teaching, writing, traveling together. Always together. We would often count our blessings that this lifestyle had been possible. Fatigued by travel, we were fatigued together. Delighted by a successful lecture, we were delighted together. No more. This easy mutuality, a gift given rather than a skill acquired, was now taking leave of our marriage.

And I could sense the distance creeping into our relationship. Because she would not remember what I wanted to tell her, I was tempted to not even mention it. She won't remember it anyway. But this temptation would lead to less and less communication. I decided to share this idea or information anyway—for my own sake and trusting that something was coming through in the words shared. Her remembering was no longer the point.

* * * *

Evelyn died at 4:00 AM on November 16, 2020. Two days later in a private ceremony (due to Covid concerns) we returned her to the earth. Prayers were shared among the dozen who attended as we lowered her cardboard coffin, with neither embalming nor cremation, into the ground. It was as simple as she would have wanted. We had married on a very cold January day in 1970; now fifty years and ten months later on a very cold day in November we buried my beloved.

When your lover dies, the world goes dark. What to do? Call or write dear friends with the sad news. They respond, remembering your partner in ways that increases the pain, but then they recall parts of Evelyn that I had lost sight of or had taken for granted.

Seeking out Evelyn I first see her face, pain-free and lovely in death. Then I try to look past that precious moment to the person I lived with, worked with for fifty years. But I am stopped by the last few years when her memory loss left her drained of much of her vitality. I push past these sober thoughts, searching for the girl in those earlier decades of full vigor. And I read the letters from those whose lives had been touched, altered by her presence to them.

Then a world of grace opens up. Several mentioned her posture. Women loved how she carried herself. No one else walked that upright. And this was more than physical; there was a moral posture that was wholly attractive. A long-time friend wrote, "We can still hear Evelyn's voice from days gone by, so precise, so composed, so joyous. That gift will not be lost." Another wrote, "My memory is of her vivaciousness, brilliance and commitment

. . . and the two of you so bonded and looking in the same direction."

The biggest surprise in these letters was the number of women who found Evelyn a powerful mentor. These individuals were often ten or even twenty years younger than Evelyn. They had met a woman who was unapologically herself moving through her days with exceptional grace.

A junior colleague wrote, "Meeting you, Evelyn, a joyful female intellectual, was a revelation to me. You somehow gave me permission to have questions and to pursue those questions. That experience of permission was pivotal in my life and career." Yet another younger woman: "Delight, hospitality, faithfulness—your modeling of these was and continues to be a profound gift in my life."

These remarks awakened signature moments in our years of public speaking. While writing together a book on marriage we came across the observation of how many women marry then "diminish into a wife." Everyone could see that Evelyn was nobody's "wife."

My only moment of doubt arose early in our relationship when she casually mentioned that she had decided not to marry, so far finding no one she ambitioned spending her life with. I pondered the remark in my heart, then muttered to myself, "we will see."

Early in our shared career we were discussing with other faculty and students at the Institute for Pastoral Studies at Loyola some question about the style of adult exchange we were attempting. As the meeting came to a close, a woman entered the room, remarking that she had wanted to join the meeting but had remained outside the door, unsure if she was welcome. Evelyn turned to her and responded with great energy, "Go through the door!"

Everyone was startled at the forcefulness of her response. Evelyn was speaking of all the doors that women had stood outside of, assuming they were locked.

Words of Appreciation from China

Our years of teaching in China left young scholars there with potent memories of Evelyn. Since her death, friends and colleagues have gathered memories of her and published them on a Chinese website, www.xinde.org (*xinde* means "faith," as in the Catholic Faith Press, which manages the website. Some contributions can be read in English translation).

Bishop Thaddeus Ma Da Qin recalled meeting Evelyn at the Guang Xi Press when he was editor there. "She gave me the impression that she was very amiable and demure. I thought of the Chinese saying, 'Sincerity inside, courtesy outside.' She and James helped the Press secure new computers and also arranged for copyrights for several important books, including their own. Now Evelyn—God's good daughter—returns to her heavenly Father and lives in God's garden forever. I was so pleased to get to know her and James."

Professor Zhang Qing Xiong, who first invited the Whiteheads to Fudan University, wrote: "During their years of teaching at Fudan, Evelyn and James won the respect of teachers and students for their profound knowledge, modest behavior, and outstanding teaching. Their lecturing together was a new experience at Fudan; their style was to patiently urge and guide students to participate in the discussion and ask questions. I was fortunately able to audit many of their lectures and learned a great deal from them. Their words were like flowing clouds or a spring breeze, and the students' ears were fully immersed in the melodious sound.

"Their teaching has helped establish the foundation for the psychology of religion, the sociology of religion and the comparative study of religion in the Academic Department of Religion at Fudan University."

Rachel Zhu Xiao Hong, a young professor in the philosophy department who often translated for the Whitehead's lectures, recalled how "their joint classes captured the hearts of the students. They seemed to bring out the best in each other and their lectures were very down to earth." She added, "Evelyn was the one most people have never seen: a respected professor with perfect gray hair and also a kind grandmother."

Rachel recalls that when her family was on sabbatical in South Bend, Evelyn would even crawl under the table to play with Ivan, their five-year-old son. She would read to him from a book on Thomas the Train and listen as he explained the "parking lot" he was designing on a large white paper.

Our colleague at Fudan, Professor Fan Lizhu, wrote, "Their gift to me was not only their support for a young scholar but their respect for the Chinese culture and their commitment to an academic comparison of East and West. Over ten years of cooperation the three of us published a series of bilingual textbooks on the sociology of religion. Jim and Evelyn were Catholic but showed a broad interest in questions of human destiny. They were not only colleagues but became family members."

A Catholic graduate student wrote, "In my conversion journey several women played key roles, and Evelyn was one of those. Her vitality never seemed to be exhausted. It seemed to come from the grace of God, and Evelyn helped us touch it and feel it.

"In Evelyn I saw a woman who was an absolute equal to her husband but without losing her feminine gentleness. Both Evelyn and James generously helped me and my husband edit our dissertations. I will never forget Evelyn's passionate and powerful voice and Jim's steady and comforting gaze."

* * *

But for a Broken Hip

Did I mention my stroke? It all began with a broken hip. The patio chair I was wrestling with looked too large for the narrow side door in the garage. Maybe I could force it through. The next sensation was hitting the pavement with hip-fracturing velocity.

At the hospital the next day X-rays showed it was a clean break that three pins would secure. But the X-rays also showed a troubled heart with an aorta in dire need of repair. The repair of hip went forward, and I was told to talk with a cardiologist soon.

When I finally consulted the physician it was late November, weeks after Evelyn, my wife of fifty years, had died of lung cancer. I felt little incentive to repair a fractured heart. The physician was empathic and acknowledged that such surgery at age eighty-two was perilous. The surgeon I consulted emphasized the difficulty of the operation and said I had to be up for a fight. But I had no fight left in me.

I left the consultation deciding not to have the surgery. My friends would have none of it. One pointed out that "fight" was the surgeon's metaphor; it need not be mine. Why not instead of "fight," we think of choosing life?

So early on the morning of April 12, 2021, I entered Memorial Hospital in South Bend, Indiana. The aorta was repaired with some effort, but in the strain of things I suffered a mild stroke on my right side. During rehab I was wheeled one day into a small gathering of stroke victims; what was I, the heart patient, doing amid these afflicted? It took some effort to realize I was one of them.

A Little Shop of Horrors

The first days after surgery were horrible. Drug-induced hallucinations raced through my mind. I was convinced the surgery had taken place in Moscow; the next night the venue had shifted to Toronto. The nurses were not pleased. They wanted another answer to the question, "Do you know where you are?" So eventually I lied to them. "We are in Memorial Hospital in South Bend." They breathed a sigh of relief.

Another torment was the face mask that gave me oxygen. I was convinced it was suffocating me and tried repeatedly to remove it. Again disfavor from the nurses; I was outstaying my welcome.

The horrors of the first week lessened, and I slipped into several weeks of restless sleeping, overwhelming fatigue, and the puzzle of nighttime continence. I had once known how that worked.

For months, or so it seemed, I had no interest in anything. The beloved *New York Times* lay there on the bed, unread. I had no concentration. If I tried to read, my energy collapsed almost immediately. Stamina was in low supply. I was busy staying alive. I was not depressed; that would have taken too much energy. Morning oatmeal was the hit of the menu. At 7:00 PM I was falling asleep.

Two beloved friends kept daily vigil, smuggling in doughnuts and Starbucks coffee in place of the coffee-like liquid from the hospital. They pampered me, keeping me alive.

So ended the month in the hospital as I learned to get out of bed without using my arms (respecting what is called the sternal precaution, not disturbing the sternum that had been recently stapled together). The second month began with my return home, wheelchair-bound.

Three kinds of outpatient therapy ensued: occupational (pull up your socks); cognitive (what did you just ask me?); and physical (stand up straight). We passed into the third month, leaving the wheelchair in favor of a walker. Then the walker was taken away, and I was told to ambulate. A therapist held the gait-belt around my waist and off I went, imitating a drunken sailor. Then the walk slowly improved, as though an ancient memory was being recalled.

The Light in My Office Was On

Most days I made due sitting in the recliner in our living room. From there I could see my office, which seemed dark and distant. Then one day I noticed the light was on. Turning on the computer I found that my right hand had forgotten how to type. I was told that in a week or two—it was true—it would remember.

And so began a gradual and miraculous recovery. Each few days I would notice a new interest in something I had been working on. And more energy to pay attention to it for a half hour. The brain was slowly recalling what it used to know by heart.

If not for a broken hip I would not have learned of a fractured heart, which found repair and has allowed me to write this memoir.

Near the end, just the two of us and the weeping willow

Epilogue

When we had been married only a decade Doubleday invited us to write a book about marriage. Foolishly we agreed. It went well. Two decades later we returned to this theme. Then again two decades later our friend and colleague Ed Foley invited us to contribute to the book he was editing, Catholic Marriage: A Pastoral and Liturgical Commentary, *published by Liturgical Training Publications in 2021. This was the last essay we wrote together.*

Promises to Keep: A Spirituality of Christian Marriage

James and Evelyn Whitehead

In his reflection on the vital energy of *eros,* Pope Benedict XVI describes "that love between man and woman which is neither planned nor willed, but somehow imposes itself upon human beings" (*God Is Love,* §3). This experience of love is often registered initially as romance—a charged delight that draws a couple together, offering the promise of a richer, shared life.

"What does she possibly see in him?" To this query of friends and relatives, two answers come to mind. "Love is blind" and "Only the lover has eyes to see." Romance is the season of lovely illusions that often serve worthy purposes, coaxing us to shed our well-defended independence and chronic preference for doing things our own way. We do not realize—we need not yet realize—the differences, conflicts, and renegotiations that will hone our romance into something real and lasting, into a sacrament.

Writers vie to describe the charming perils of romance. Roberto Unger: "The lover must suspend the defensive aloofness that marks so much of his experience in society. He must run the risk of being rebuffed or disappointed. He must expose himself to perilous emotion and ridiculous gesture." Daring such a risk we find that falling in love "always has something of the miraculous. It is an act of grace." In Marilynne Robinson's prize-winning novel *Gilead*, a widowed minister, surprised by love, marvels at the force of such affection. "That there should be a voice in the whole world, and that I should be the one to hear it, seemed to me then and seems to me now an unfathomable grace." Both authors celebrate romance as a grace.

The ignition of romance, whether we are young or old, is marked by infatuation: a person becomes utterly enchanted by another. Everything about the other person is engrossing, and little beyond this relationship seems important. In this timeless present of romance *you and I* are all there is. The world tends to be tolerant of this attitude in lovers, at least for a while. We know this shared obsession is but a phase of romance. The romance will mature into a deeper love or die from lack of any further substance. Soon the lovers will rejoin us—better, we trust, for the experience.

Sometimes as jaded adults we may look back on such youthful enchantment as a season of immaturity and blind romance. Bruised or simply more experienced at life, we feel far removed from that disruptive erotic force that stirred us long ago. Yet psychologists remind us that infatuation is itself an achievement. In romance a young person comes to prize another as both a focus of sexual attraction and emotional care. Passion and tenderness are joined, often for the first time, in the young person's heart. The beloved becomes more than a target of one's desire or an object of passion. Romance deepens as we not only relish occasional sojourns in the other's company. Now we want more; we want to spend our life together.

If love, begun in high romance, is to last, our illusions must be confronted. This demands not the repudiation of romance, but its purification. This purification is expressed in commitment and fidelity.

Commitment

In the commitments of marriage we promise ourselves for the future—a time that stretches out beyond our control. We pledge our future based only on what we know now. We are promising to hold ourselves accountable to do "whatever is necessary" to make this promise happen. We are building a stable place where our passion can grow and bear fruit.

The future is sure to bring changes; how can we guarantee that this commitment will last, that our promises will be worth keeping? Such vital engagements come without warranty, yet if we cannot pledge ourselves in this risky fashion we will remain alone and our lives will less likely bear fruit.

In many ways it is these promises that transform our early attraction into marriage—an enduring relationship of mutual love and shared life-giving. Through the hopes we hold for our life together we condition the future—we begin to mold and shape it. We open ourselves to possibilities, we make demands, we place limits, we hold one another in trust.

In the early commitments of marriage—to attention, affection, responsibility—we begin to practice the virtue of intimacy. We learn the physical and emotional nuances that render lovemaking special for us. We discover the ways in which passion and affection, humor and intensity, are part of our own love life. Loving me in my body, you invite me beyond shame and guilt I may still carry. With you I am free to explore my passion and to expose my vulnerability and self-doubt. Having risked the self-revelation of sex, we can approach with greater confidence the often more threatening process of self-disclosure upon which the quality of our life together will depend.

Exposing our bodies to one another is one thing; exposing our vulnerability and hesitations to each other may be more challenging. Are we sure enough about ourselves to risk drawing this close to another person? Are we open to being revealed to ourself—our generosity and petulance, our humor and our self-doubt?

The personal strength of intimacy includes the capacity to commit myself to a particular person, in a relationship that lasts over time, and to meet the accompanying demands for change, in ways that do not compromise my own integrity. In the early years of marriage we discover the particularity—that is, the peculiarity—of our spouse. This is the person we love, not some idealized version of a spouse. And we are mutually committed for the long term; beyond the flush of romance, other skills and resources will be necessary to keep us united. And we are learning to compromise—a dirty word to the young romantic. We discover how compromise and personal integrity can abide together in this love relationship. The strength and virtue of intimacy means learning to live with both the exhilaration and the strain of sharing life with another person.

In these first years of marriage we learn about the rhythm of saying *yes* and saying *no*. Every life commitment takes root in the capacity to say just a few *yeses*—to this person, to this career path, to this lifestyle—and surrounding these affirmations with dozens of *nos*: bidding adieu to paths not taken and turning from distractions whose initial charm is more deception than gift.

Fidelity

The commitments that give shape to our marriage and the emerging virtue of intimacy gradually mature into the psychological strength and virtue of *fidelity:* the capacity to sustain loyalties that have been freely pledged, in the face of inevitable contradictions that arise in any ongoing relationship. Fidelity does not insure that we will never experience difficulty or conflict in our overlapping lives. Fidelity does not suggest that we will never let one another down. But fidelity makes mature love possible. We learn not only to make promises, but to keep them.

This psychological resource stabilizes us so that we can continue to honor our freely pledged loyalty—acknowledging the complications that are part of our past, the hesitancies that remain active in the present, and problems that will inevitably confront us in our future together. With frustrating regularity, we let each other down. But we also learn to begin again, to forgive and to accept forgiveness. We gradually shed the illusions and expectations that were perhaps previously necessary, but now have become burdensome.

The most mature gift of fidelity is its flexibility. "You are not the person I married!" Indeed. We are committed to a person who keeps growing and changing, as we do ourselves. So our fidelity is not just to promises once made in youthful enthusiasm, but to a shared journey. Along the way we are revealed ever more deeply to ourselves, even as we continue to learn about our partner. Gradually we recognize that our life's vocation is not a single call, but a life-long conversation with God.

The virtue of mutuality emerges in the everyday conversations of how to merge our various gifts and concerns. It is here that we craft the authority of our married love. Learning when and how to compromise, we come to see that compromise is often the way to say I love you.

Generative Love: From "We Are" to "We Care"

Love is creative beyond itself, and it must be so if it is to endure. A love that does not open us to wider concerns risks becoming a caricature of intimacy. Love that does not give life beyond itself will die; Christian wisdom has long proclaimed this sometimes fleeting insight from our own experience. There is an essential connection between loving and giving life. It is this abiding truth that the church tries to share in its celebration of the fruitfulness of marriage.

The special magic of love is that it desires to make more of itself. "Making love" we make more life—between us and beyond us. When our love generates new life in children, we are astonished and grateful. This is more than our doing! If we are still very young we may see this new life as a *reproduction*—a new version of us. Then we learn the mellow lesson of fruitfulness: this *reproduction* is very different from us, a separate person with new dreams and unheard-of plans. Our child is a gift of God to the world, but we were there to help it happen.

In every marriage the partners hope to be fruitful: to have their lives mean something special, to leave a mark, make a contribution. For many centuries fruitfulness was simply pictured as biological fecundity. To be fruitful meant to have many children. Yet we all know married couples who have reproduced many offspring, but whose lives seem pinched and ungenerous. And we know childless couples who contribute greatly to their community in works of justice and compassion.

Marriage involves balancing the tensions between our intimacy as a couple and the larger responsibilities of our lives. The challenge is to expand the scope of our effective concern. The birth of our first child can be an early challenge. Here we may experience some strain, as we learn to expand beyond ourselves as a couple, in ways that do not erode the commitments of mutuality between us. Job responsibilities and career choices also raise the challenge. Does marriage mean that only one of us may pursue a career? How do I, how do we, manage the multiple demands of being responsible citizen, financial provider, parent, and spouse? The question can surface as an issue of social concern. How do we balance our commitments to each other and to our children alongside our responsibility to the needs of the world?

An early exclusive focus in love is normal, an important dynamic of the process of exploration and self-disclosure that contributes to the possibility of commitment. But maturing love moderates this exclusivity. Being *for* one another does not require that we have no concern for anyone else. Indeed, the enrichment we experience in being for one another leads us to be for more than *just us*. Our love gives us more of what is best in each of us. We feel the impetus to move beyond ourselves, to bring others into the power of what our love has given us. This movement of expansion is an expected dynamic of love as it matures.

Psychologists are aware of the importance to our love of this impulse beyond ourselves. They warn that the absence of any movement beyond *just us* imperils a love relationship. A "pseudo-intimacy" may result, turning the partners in upon themselves in ways that gradually impoverishes the relationship. What results from this failure to expand our concern is not an intimacy more protected and complete, but stagnation.

The Practice of Christian Marriage

Marriage, we quickly learn, takes practice. Not that we should try it several times in order to get it right. Rather, this relationship, in order to survive and flourish, demands regular attention—daily practices of affection, patience, and reconciliation. Theologians and spiritual guides are returning today to the notion of "practices"—intentional actions, performed again and again, and done for their own sake. Julie Hanlon Rubio provides a comprehensive definition: "an intentional, shared action, situated in the context of a tradition, ordinary in outward appearances but transcendent in its association with fundamental human goods."

Rubio, in her study of family life, explores a number of intentional practices—ranging from the couples' pattern of love-making to the family eating together—that she calls "practices of resistance." These repeated activities are meant to resist cultural forces around sex, food, and obsessive consumption that may well distort a Christian family's values.

An important early practice in marriage we might call "the clarification of expectations." When we marry we bring with us a rich and complex set of assumptions of what marriage "should look like." These assumptions are often unspoken, perhaps even to ourselves. They have been inherited from our parents and family, from our Christian education and from the depictions of marriage in our culture. We think we "know" what a marriage is, how husbands and wives are supposed to act, how children are to be raised. Some of these expectations are good and valuable; others may be destructive or simply inappropriate to our own marriage. They are often more someone else's expectations than our own, but they are the inheritance we bring to our marriage.

As our marriage strengthens, we come into a deeper knowledge of who we are together. We begin the necessary process of reflecting together on our expectations and evaluating that fit our life together and that do not. This process is the journey into the authority and uniqueness of our own marriage.

We may, for example, bring with us the conviction that conflict has no place in our relationship. Our assumption has been that conflict is destructive and always wrong.

We have not experienced healthy models of dealing with conflict in either our marriage or our faith community. When conflict does arise, as it must, we are confused and depressed. We may well be tempted to simply refuse to face any conflict, hoping that our ignoring it will make it go away. Or, if we are blessed, we may come to see that conflict can serve as a portal to an enriching of our love. In a risky but healthy response to conflict we lay bare our vulnerability and fear. We trust each other to hold this fragility with compassion. Our memory of biblical conflicts helps here: Jacob wrestling with a nocturnal adversary until it finally dawned on him that his opponent was his God (Genesis 32); Paul and Peter strongly disagreeing about the requirements of membership in the early church, until they agreed to disagree (Galatians 3). In these sacred stories and our own lives we begin to learn that conflict is one of the ways we hold the people we love.

Another expectation brought with us into our marriage was, perhaps, that we would each fully satisfy every need of the other. Friend, lover, companion: our mutual love was such that neither of us would ever need others. As our marriage matures, we learn that this is not so. We cannot, and need not, be all things to each other. This recognition does not herald the end of our generous loving; it is more the purifying of an earlier romantic expectation that we now realize does not serve our love.

The Lifestyle of Marriage

The practices of marriage are forged in the contexts of the couple's lifestyle. Marriage celebrates love, marriage includes commitment; marriage also creates a lifestyle—

not a single pattern experienced universally but many particular lifestyles through which married couples express their love and live out the promises that hold them in mutual care.

The lifestyle of marriage is the pattern of our life together, a design that emerges in the choices we make. Many people do not experience the patterns of their daily life as open to personal choice. By the time of marriage, and from long before, factors of poverty or class or personality have narrowed the life circumstances over which they have much say. But most Americans today experience a heightened consciousness of choice. We are aware that there are different ways in which the possibilities of life and of marriage may be lived out. And while our choices are always limited, we are aware that we not only can but must choose among these options for ourselves. The lifestyle of our marriage thus results from both our choices and our circumstances.

The choices that construct the lifestyle of our marriage include the decisions we make about the practical details of living—the routine of our daily activities, how we allocate the current tasks of family and household care. But more basic decisions are involved—the values we hold important, the goals we have for our life together, the ways we choose to invest ourselves in the world.

Today there is more choice involved in the link between marriage and parenthood. Couples come to the decision to have a child with more consideration given to how many children there shall be in the family, how the birth of these children shall be spaced, when in marriage the commitments of family life shall begin. Some couples who have been unable to give birth to children seek other ways to expand their life together as a family—often through adoption or foster care. Other couples decide not to have a family—and instead, to express their love beyond themselves in other forms of creativity and care.

A comparable challenge accompanies each of these options—to develop a way of being together in marriage that takes seriously the demands of mutuality in our own relationship, as it takes seriously the challenge that we look beyond ourselves in genuine contribution and care. How shall we give and nurture life beyond ourselves: in our own children? In our friendships and other relationships? In our creative work? In our generous concern for the world? And the decisions that we come to here do much to determine the design of our daily life together.

Beyond this central choice concerning the focus of our creative love, other decisions about lifestyle confront us. How shall we use the resources we possess? How, especially, do we allocate our money and our time? Here again the questions can be stated simply: What is our money for? What has priority in our use of time? We can respond to these questions at the practical level, offering the balance sheet of the family budget and our calendar of weekly events. But as an issue in lifestyle the question goes more to the core: How are our own deepest values expressed or obscured in how we spend our money and our time?

Most American families today experience both money and time as scarce. There is not enough of either to go around. We have little discretionary income and even less free time. There seem to be more possibilities, more demands than we feel we can meet. But among the demands that seem both genuine and inevitable there are others that seem to squander us uselessly, leaving us no time to be together or to be at peace and leaving us few resources to use for any purpose beyond ourselves. This sense of overextension characterizes the lifestyle of many marriages. Its prevalence invites us to reflect on our own patterns of money and time. The goal of this kind of reflection is not looking to praise or blame but trying to come to a better sense of the motives and pressures that move us and, in that way, define our lives.

Establishing our lifestyle in marriage is not done once and for all; this is itself an ongoing process. The lifestyle of our marriage must respond to the movements of development and change in each of us, in our relationship and in our responsibilities. Marriage for a lifetime, then, develops through the interaction of our relationship, our commitments, and our lifestyle. Our mutual love is at the core of marriage. But in marriage we experience our relationship as more than just our love here and now.

Devotion

Devotion is the most extravagant blessing born of maturing love. This strength anchors an abiding commitment, rooted in appreciation that someone else's well-being is as important to me as is my own. Here again, we move beyond a general love of humanity. Devotion arises in our relationships with *particular* persons. And devotion expands when the experience is mutual; I, too, am held in this treasured embrace. The greatest gift of devoted relationships is presence—the promise that we will *be there* for one another, the assurance that we will not be abandoned.

Devotion is love that is *well aged*. Accustomed over decades to each other's ways—both the endearing and the maddening—we know each other well. The youthful passion of romance has been transmuted into the tender-ness that enjoys growing old together.

In time, the shape of aging love earns the name of devotion. Devotion is the enfleshed affection that sur-vives illness and aging and enjoys growing old together. The first-century author Plutarch wrote: "The love for a virtuous woman suffers no autumn but flourishes even with grey hair and wrinkles." By this point child-rearing is long gone; active careers are over; the couple's love becomes an affection nuanced by the awareness of final days, threatening illness. Such devotion might be called *eros* with wrinkles.

Another, more dramatic story of devotion appeared in the final days of the British philosopher and novelist Iris Murdoch. Her husband, John Bayley, writes, in *Elegy for Iris*, of the months of caring for a mate suffering the rav-ages of Alzheimer's disease. "After more than forty years of taking our marriage for granted, marriage has decided it is tired of this and is taking a hand in the game. Pur-posefully, persistently, involuntarily, our marriage is now getting somewhere. It is giving us no choice, and I am glad of it."

A spirituality of Christian marriage is bold enough to compare the fragile affection we share with another human to the affection that binds us to our Creator. Mari-lynne Robinson has her aging minister in the novel *Gilead* muse on this comparison of the "love of God with mortal love. But I just can't see them as separate things at all. If we can be divinely fed with a morsel and divinely blessed with a touch, then the terrible pleasure we find in a par-ticular face can certainly instruct us in the nature of the very grandest love."

Bibliography

A. Whitehead Books and Essays, Chronologically

1979   *Christian Life Patterns: The Psychological Challenges and Religious Invitations of Adult Life.* New York: Doubleday.

1981   *Marrying Well: Possibilities in Christian Marriage Today.* New York: Doubleday.

1981   *Method in Ministry: Theological Reflection and Christian Ministry.* Minneapolis: Winston-Seabury.

1982   *Community of Faith: Models and Strategies for Developing Christian Communities.* Minneapolis: Winston-Seabury.

1983   "Passages in Homosexual Holiness." In *A Challenge to Love: Gay and Lesbian Catholics in the Church.* Edited by Robert Nugent. New York: Crossroad.

1984   *Seasons of Strength: New Visions of Adult Christian Maturing.* New York: Doubleday Image.

1986   *The Emerging Laity: Returning Leadership to the Community of Faith.* New York: Doubleday Image.

1987   "The Shape of Compassion: Catholics and Homosexuality." *Spirituality Today* 39, no. 2 (Summer): 126–35.

1989   *A Sense of Sexuality: Christian Love and Intimacy.* New York: Crossroad.

1991   *The Promise of Partnership: A Model for Collaborative Ministry.* New York: HarperCollins Publishers.

1992   *Christians and Their Passions.* Warren Lecture Series in Catholic Studies 21. The University of Tulsa.

1994   *Shadows of the Heart: A Spirituality of the Painful Emotions.* New York: Crossroad.

1998   "Making a Living; Making a Life." *New Theology Review* 11, no. 3 (August): 5-13.

2001   *Wisdom of the Body. Making Sense of our Sexuality.* New York: Crossroad.

2004   With Fan Lizhu. "Fate and Fortune: Popular Religion and Moral Capital in Shenzhen." *Journal of Chinese Religions* 32: 83–100.

2005   With Fan Lizhu. "The Spiritual Search in Shenzhen: Adopting and Adapting China's Common Spiritual Heritage." *Nova Religio* 9, no. 2, 50-61.

2006   With Fan Lizhu. *Religion in the Late-Modern World.* Beijing: Current Affairs Press.

2009   *Holy Eros: Pathways to a Passionate God.* Maryknoll, NY: Orbis Books.

2010   *Transforming Painful Emotions.* Maryknoll, NY: Orbis Books.

2010   With Fan Lizhu. *Sociology of Religion: Religion and China.* Beijing: Current Affairs Press.

2011   With Fan Lizhu. "Spirituality in a Modern Chinese Metropolis." In *Chinese Religious Life.* Edited by David Palmer, Glenn Shive, and Philip L. Wickeri. Oxford: Oxford University Press, 13–29.

2012   *Nourishing the Spirit: The Healing Emotions of Wonder, Joy, Compassion and Hope.* Maryknoll, NY: Orbis Books.

2012   With Fan Lizhu. *China and the Cultural Sociology of Religion.* Beijing: Current Affairs Press.

2014   *Fruitful Embraces: Sexuality, Love and Justice.* New York: iUniverse.

2016   *The Virtue of Resilience*. Maryknoll, NY: Orbis Books.

2018   *Enchanting the World*: *The Vision of Twentieth-Century Catholic Writers*. New York: Crossroad.

2019   "Promises to Keep: A Spirituality of Christian Marriage." In *Catholic Marriage*. Edited by Edward Foley. Chicago: Liturgical Training Publications.

2020   *Make Holy These Gifts*: *Enchantment and the Catholic Faith*. New York: Crossroad.

2021   *The Grace of Enchantment*: *Appreciating the World as Sacrament*. Amazon.

B. Most Influential Secondary Sources

Dupré, Louis

   1993   *Passage to Modernity*: *An Essay in the Hermeneutics of Nature and Culture*. New Haven, CT: Yale University Press.

Erikson, Erik

   1963   *Childhood and Society*. New York: Norton.

   1968   *Identity: Youth and Crisis*. New York: Norton.

Levinson, Daniel

   1978   *The Seasons of a Man's Life*. New York: Knopf.

MacIntyre, Alisdair

   1981   *After Virtue*. South Bend, IN: Notre Dame University Press.

Nussbaum, Martha

   2001   *Upheavals of Thought. The Intelligence of Emotions*. Cambridge: Cambridge University Press.

Schjeldahl, Peter

   2003   "El Greco at the Met." In *The New Yorker*, October 20, 198.

Sheehy, Gail
  1976   *Passages: Predictable Crises of Adult Life.* New York: Dutton.
Steiner, George
  1989   *Real Presences.* Chicago: University of Chicago Press.
Taylor, Charles
  2007   *A Secular Age.* Cambridge, MA: Harvard University Press.
Tracy, David
  1988   *Plurality and Ambiguity.* San Francisco: Harper & Row.
Unger, Roberto
  1984   *Passion: An Essay on Personality.* New York: Free Press.
Vaillant, George
  1977   *Adaptation to Life.* Boston: Little Brown.

Notes on Authors

Evelyn Eaton Whitehead (PhD, University of Chicago in Human Development) and James Whitehead (PhD, Harvard University in World Religions) met in 1961 at St. Louis University when they began graduate studies in philosophy.

They married in January 1970, and James began teaching at the Institute of Pastoral Studies at Loyola University in Chicago that summer. They both taught as adjunct faculty there from the early 1970s to 2015, while also teaching in the Theology Department at the University of Notre Dame from 1973 to 1978.

In 1992 they served as Warren Professors at the University of Tulsa and in 1998 began teaching fall semesters at Fudan University in Shanghai, China. During the early 2000s they also lectured each spring at several educational programs in Hong Kong.

In 2004 they were awarded honorary degrees in Doctor of Ministry at Catholic Theological Union in Chicago. In 2017 they received the *Aggiornamento* Award from the Institute of Pastoral Studies, Loyola University Chicago.

Their work has been translated into seven languages.

Made in the USA
Columbia, SC
22 August 2022

65183491R00080